WORKOUT & GROW RICH

WORKOUT & GROW RICH

Connecting the Dots Between HEALTH and WEALTH

PERRY LIEBER

New York

WORKOUT & GROW RICH
Connecting the Dots Between HEALTH and WEALTH

Published in New York, New York, by Morgan James Publishing. Morgan James and The Entrepreneurial Publisher are trademarks of Morgan James, LLC. www.MorganJamesPublishing.com

The Morgan James Speakers Group can bring authors to your live event. For more information or to book an event visit The Morgan James Speakers Group at www.TheMorganJamesSpeakersGroup.com.

Shelfie

A **free** eBook edition is available with the purchase of this print book.

CLEARLY PRINT YOUR NAME ABOVE IN UPPER CASE

Instructions to claim your free eBook edition:
1. Download the Shelfie app for Android or iOS
2. Write your name in **UPPER CASE** above
3. Use the Shelfie app to submit a photo
4. Download your eBook to any device

ISBN 978-1-63047-718-9 paperback
ISBN 978-1-63047-719-6 eBook
Library of Congress Control Number:
2015911996

Cover Design by:
Rachel Lopez
www.r2cdesign.com

Interior Design by:
Bonnie Bushman
The Whole Caboodle Graphic Design

In an effort to support local communities and raise awareness and funds, Morgan James Publishing donates a percentage of all book sales for the life of each book to Habitat for Humanity Peninsula and Greater Williamsburg.

Get involved today, visit
www.MorganJamesBuilds.com

Habitat
for Humanity®
Peninsula and
Greater Williamsburg
Building Partner

To my beautiful wife, Nora, and our lovely daughter, Sage.
And to all my clients, friends, and mentors
who have helped me put this project together.

CONTENTS

FOREWORD

I met Perry Lieber in 2006 when he was a trainer working with my thirteen-year-old son, who was suffering from femoral retroversion (knowing I'd need a simple explanation, my wife told me it was a hip problem affecting his gait). Perry's concern for physical well-being and the effect it has on emotional well-being was evident even then. My son made rapid progress, and today he has no noticeable problems with this condition. Apart from knowing what my son needed to do, I knew that any trainer who had the patience and ability to get this particular son to actually work out a couple of days a week was someone worth knowing. In this respect, I was absolutely right.

Over the next couple of years, Perry increasingly became a part of our family's efforts to stay active and healthy. Soon he was training my very athletic wife. Over time, he began training her far-less athletic husband.

I've been doing some form of working out since I was about thirty. At that time, something changed (my metabolism). I could no longer eat everything in sight without gaining weight, and I was increasingly less energetic. A friend introduced me to the then very alien concept of jogging. I was stunned by the difference in my physical and mental well-being after I took up the sport.

However, by the time I was sixty, after years of jogging to keep my energy levels up and my weight down while otherwise sitting in meetings and at my desk, my back was telling me it was time to adjust my routine. I had back surgery and believed my jogging days were over. This was a problem as jogging was really the only workout I enjoyed that kept my weight and heart rate down while both energizing and calming me. I truly did my best thinking while jogging.

Although himself a fit young man who competed at the Ironman level, Perry understood that my needs were somewhat different—more at the tinman level. Immediately, he started me on the path to better balanced approaches to exercise and general health. He convinced me (no easy task) to try what he suggested and taught me stretching and core exercises that I do religiously every morning to this day. I'm still jogging and working out at age sixty-five. He deserves a lot of the credit (I have to do the exercises myself, but I'll give him the rest of the credit).

A couple of months ago, Perry asked me to review a draft of his book, *Work Out and Grow Rich*. As I read, it immediately became obvious why he had been asking me all those questions about how to succeed when training me. At the time I thought he was seeking my sage advice because he wanted to invest in his own gym and become a successful small business owner. Initially, that may even have been the case and, in fact, he did invest in a gym and is now a successful small business owner. But, reading his book, I humbly realized that I wasn't the only person with whom Perry had been having such discussions. He'd been having similar talks with other successful people he trained—corporate executives, athletes, and innovators. These were not just financially successful people, but people who had managed to succeed and have fulfilling personal lives.

In the course of these discussions, he received insights into what he needed to do to be successful as well as broader perspectives on how a person's physical well-being could be a major contributor to personal and financial success. More specifically, he heard how many (if not all) of the successful people he trained considered physical well-being an essential element of their own personal and financial success.

As just about any successful person will tell you, when you feel better, you think more clearly, you focus more acutely, and you have the energy to stand up to the competition. I am personally committed to this notion. While I run a restaurant company, our three corporate offices have no cafeterias. If people want a restaurant lunch, they should at least take a walk. However, each office does have a fully equipped gym and a trainer available to all employees. We also have other programs that encourage good health. I encourage all of our executive team to work out (which does not include golf). I believe our employees are more productive and better off in their personal lives because of it.

As Perry's book lays out in easy reading detail, if you want to succeed in life, if you want to maintain success and live long enough to enjoy it, work out. Working out won't guarantee you success, but it's hard to imagine most people achieving or sustaining their success without it. While I have long held this belief personally, I found the interviews and insights in Perry's book enlightening, confirming, and, quite honestly, fascinating. The workout routines are, of course, Perry's specialty and well worth the effort.

While there are any number of books out there on how to succeed in life, Perry's is the first one I've seen that uses the personal experiences of real people who have employed a well-balanced workout routine to improve their lives and move them along the road to success. Perry's entrepreneurial instincts, his focus on physical training, and the time he's spent talking to and working out with individuals who have achieved this balance, make his book not only a truly beneficial addition to the writings on success and personal happiness, but also a very readable and compelling one.

Andy Puzder
CEO, CKE Restaurants, Inc.

Introduction
WHY WORKING OUT MAY BE YOUR SECRET TO SUCCESS

Have you ever wondered what it would take for you to be really successful in life? Not just earn a lot of money, or love what you do, or have great relationships, or be in top physical condition—but to have it *all*?

Maybe that sounds too good to be true. Or even impossible.

For example, does this scenario sound familiar?

A thirty-three-year-old executive has a great position in a growing global corporation. She's worked hard to get to where she is, and from the outside looking in, she's on the fast track to success. As her work responsibilities grow, she starts to put her personal needs aside and to work longer and longer hours. She stops making time to work out and eat right in order to keep up and get ahead. After all, that's what it takes to be successful, right?

Wrong! Ignoring your personal health and working all day, every day, isn't the path to success at all. It's the path to burnout. As a personal trainer and workplace wellness consultant who has worked with top corporate executives, I see it all the time. Those who believe success at work requires sacrificing their personal health consistently end up being less productive, disliking their jobs, and dreading their days—and they usually have no idea why. Very often the reason is simple: they've stopped making time to work out and move their bodies the way nature intended.

Now how about this scenario?

A recent college graduate hasn't been able to find a job in his field and is waiting tables while sending out résumés. It seems that every day the media is reporting on yet another corporate scandal or the vast abyss between "the rich" or "the top 1 percent" and the rest of us. Rather than give up his principles, he keeps his minimum-wage job and assumes financial success just isn't in his future. He's given up on the possibility that he could ever become financially wealthy doing what he loves.

As I learned in this process;

Just keep on going. Don't give up. I think so many people have dreams and goals, and they want to be a success overnight. That never happens. It takes years to build brands and build people and companies. I just try to really encourage people not to give up. (Patty Aubery)

I admit that I've been very fortunate to make a great living doing what I love. For the past ten years, I've been an elite personal trainer of professional athletes, celebrities, and executives of global corporations. I also co-own a company called Foundwellness with my wife, Nora, which helps businesses incorporate workplace workouts to keep their employees and executives healthy and performing at their best. I've always loved working out, and to spend all day every day helping successful people stay fit and achieve peak performance at work has been awesome. But I also knew I had a lot to learn as a business owner.

I'm also fortunate to work with many executives, business owners, and professionals who would certainly qualify as the "rich" or the "top 1 percent" in terms of overall life success. I'm not just talking about money. They consistently find joy and meaning in their work, maintain healthy family relationships and friendships, are healthy and fit, and perform at the highest level in their work. They are rich not just financially, but in every meaningful sense of the word. Somehow they've found a way to have it all.

Inspired by *Think and Grow Rich* author Napoleon Hill, I decided to personally interview these clients to see if I could discover any common denominators to their success that could help me as I was trying to get to the next level in my own success. It didn't take long for me to learn that successful people didn't achieve success by accident. After studying hours of interview transcripts, I was able to identify several key practices they all shared.

Overall, I discovered that most of these practices were very similar to the ones Napoleon Hill wrote about in *Think and Grow Rich*, such as the importance of desire and dreaming big ("Lead from Within," chapter 5), setting meaningful goals (chapter 6), and masterminding ("Collaborate," chapter 3)—practices most success experts have been teaching for decades.

However, one habit kept coming up in every interview that isn't typically listed as a key to peak performance or success. No matter how busy they were, they all made time to work out regularly.

At first, I didn't even list working out as a success habit. As a personal trainer and competitive athlete, I take working out for granted. I love doing it (some might even say I'm obsessed with it), so it's easy for me to make time for it. Plus, it's my job. But then I started thinking about my clients, and I realized that wasn't true for a lot of them. In fact, one of them, whose story you'll read about in chapter 7, only began working out after he almost died from heart disease at age forty-one. So I added "working out" to my list of foundational success habits.

That's when I decided I had to share what I had learned. We all know that our society is becoming more and more sedentary—you don't need me to cite any statistics. Most people already know how important exercise is for personal health, but few ever make the direct connection between working out and success in work and life and therefore rarely include it as part of their success plan. It just becomes a personal development goal or something people know they "should" do that somehow never gets done.

My most successful clients know that working out is foundational for their success *at work*, as well as in life. Yes, thoughts are things, but we're more than just thoughts. Now more than ever we need a clear reminder that we were made to *move*! The physical fuels the emotional and intellectual.

Okay, I admit the title of this book is a bit of an exaggeration to get your attention. Working out isn't the *only* key to growing rich in health, wealth, happiness, and purpose (or all of the above). But it may in fact be *your* key to success, "hidden in plain sight"—particularly if you've already been trying to "do all the right things" but still find yourself on the edge of burnout. It may be the one remaining thing that makes all the difference.

Please note: I am not putting myself forward as any kind of guru, nor am I presenting a quick, easy path toward success. These seven success habits—especially working out—require dedication and perseverance. But by defining what "rich" means for you and by practicing these success habits, you will be giving yourself the best chance toward becoming rich in energy, passion, relationships, health, happiness, and yes, even money.

What Does "Rich" Mean to You?

Ultimately, success is about being happy. You have to understand what your own goals and principles are and how to pursue those consistently in a lot of different environments and challenges. Every year I sit down and check my personal, family, and business goals, see if I am achieving them or not, and reevaluate them. Being focused and not letting a lot of outside influences come in and disrupt whatever you are doing in today's ability to communicate 24/7 is a challenge.

The above quote is from Mark Bissell, CEO of Bissell, whom you'll meet later in the book. For Mark, success is defined by happiness, and I couldn't agree more. But if success means happiness, that means no one can define what success means for you except *you*. So before we dive into what it takes to create a "rich" life, you'll need to define what a rich life means to you.

For some people, a rich life literally means becoming rich financially. For others, a rich life means helping as many people as possible through their careers or simply by volunteering their services. For still others, it means "having it all": financial wealth, a meaningful career, rich relationships, and vibrant health. Take a moment right now and define what a rich life would mean for you. If you're not sure how to do that, you could start by defining your larger purpose in life, and then write down some of your big-picture life goals that connect to that purpose. (You'll refer back to these big-picture life goals when you get to chapter 6.) Once you have a clear picture of what a rich life would be for you, you'll be ready to take full advantage of the rest of the book.

The Road Ahead

Work Out and Grow Rich has two parts. In "Part One: The Seven Healthy Habits of Success," I'll share with you the seven key work and lifestyle practices I discovered when I interviewed my most successful clients. I hope they will inspire and equip younger professionals who may not have heard them before as well as remind experienced professionals what they already know but may have forgotten. The habits are presented in the form of conversational and actionable tips so you can apply what you learn immediately. As much as possible, I've allowed them to tell you the secrets to their success in their own words.

So who are these "successful" clients? Again, all of them would be considered rich not just from a financial point of view, but in that they are living their dream.

1. Patty Aubery, president, Jack Canfield Companies
2. Ema Boateng, professional soccer player
3. Mark Bissell, CEO of Bissell
4. Will Chesebro, 2011 Team USA para-cyclist
5. Jim Corcoran, senior vice president, Morgan Stanley Wealth Management
6. Michael Fitzpatrick, tech entrepreneur and former CEO of PacTel
7. Kevin Haley, senior vice president of Innovation, Under Armour
8. Kai Lenny, world-class professional water athlete
9. Angel Martinez, CEO of Deckers Outdoor Corporation
10. Jerry Oshinsky, attorney known as the "father of insurance law"
11. Greg Renker, co-founder, Guthy-Renker, world-class direct marketing company
12. Darya Pino Rose, author and expert on the science of healthy eating
13. Ed Snider, chairman of Comcast Spectacor

Each of these individuals has his or her own unique success story that I hope will inspire you to live yours.

If Part One convinced you that working out just might be the missing piece for your success plan, Part Two will give you the practical help you need to help you immediately start incorporating working out into your routine. Why just working out and not all the success habits? I believe there are already plenty of resources available to provide more practical help for the first six habits, and I don't just want to repeat what's already out there. Beginning (and maintaining) a workout routine has unique challenges for the busy professional, and I don't see many resources directly addressing that. It's not just our sedentary Western culture working against us. Because most business cultures think of working out as a personal pursuit rather than a proven productivity booster, you're probably not going to get a ton of support at the office—especially if you're the one in charge! Plus, in my experience, success-driven people find it very difficult to find time to work out if left to their own devices, so I want to help you remove every possible excuse.

So Part Two shares detailed advice on how to eat for energy, including simple meal plans to fuel an active lifestyle, as well as my Workbody program, complete with tiered exercise plans you can begin today. It's based on the same advice I give to my own clients, including those profiled in this book, which will help you pave the path toward peak performance and workplace success.

If you've been following all the best advice from the success experts and you still haven't had the results you've expected, working out may be all you need to finally grow rich on *your* terms.

PART ONE

THE SEVEN HEALTHY
HABITS OF SUCCESS

Chapter 1
CREATE A ROUTINE

Have you ever missed a work meeting, missed a workout, showed up late for an appointment, or stayed up until two a.m. to finish a work or school project because you ran out of time? I know I've used that excuse many times: "I just didn't have time."

The truth is, we all get stressed, tired, and behind in our schedules. The reason isn't that we don't have enough time. The reason is that we're not *making* time for what's really most important. If you can learn to *make* time on a regular basis, you will become more successful, have more discretionary time, and simply be a happier person. The secret to having enough time is *creating a routine*. I know, it sounds too simple—like the way life was back in grade school. Remember grade school? Wake up, eat breakfast, go to school, play at recess, go back to class, eat lunch, return to class until school ends, go to some afterschool activity (music, sports, daycare, etc.), go home, do your homework, eat dinner, play, go to bed, repeat. Those were the good old days, when things were simple and easy.

As adults, we forget how powerful the simplicity of routine can be. There's no longer one schedule that fits all: Some people work nights, others work multiple jobs, and some people have families while others do not. So how do you create the right routine for you?

Based on what I've learned from my clients who are rich in every positive sense of the word—in health, wealth, happiness, and purpose—a successful routine includes three main components:

1. Setting boundaries
2. Setting priorities
3. Getting up early

Set Priorities

Have you ever felt overscheduled and overcommitted? We all have; it is a major cause of stress. If you often find yourself in this situation, it's a good indication that you need to set your priorities, which is the first step in creating your routine.

Mark Bissell is CEO of Bissell, a family-owned business probably best known for its vacuum cleaners and floor cleaners. Like most business owners, Mark has a lot on his plate.

I have a tendency to overschedule. I mean, I love doing things. Whether it is work related, or we get invited by friends to do really fun things, or it's working out, a year or more in advance, I start slotting things in. At the time, it makes sense. And then I think of something else, and then I think of something else, and it kind of stacks up. Every now and then, I realize, Hey, I'm overcommitted. And then I start getting stressed, which manifests itself in different ways.

I just have to step back and say, "Okay, focus. What are the three things that are important?" I do not like canceling things. If I make a commitment, I am driven to do it. But sometimes, I find that I just have to cancel. So one thing I am trying to do better with is not overscheduling. Creating more time. Because things kind of fill in as the day and the week and the month progress. If you are already scheduled half a year in advance, you know there are going to be problems.

To set his priorities, Mark says to himself, "Okay, focus. What are the three things that are important?"

What three priorities are most important to you? Mine include:

1. Family Time
2. Working out
3. Eating healthy

You might be surprised to see that "growing my business" or "becoming a top speaker" didn't make it to my top three. Why? I believe that the *physical is the foundation of the mental, emotional, and spiritual aspects of life.* So in order to be a better husband, business owner, friend, student, and trainer, I need to sweat first and keep moving (see chapter 7 for more about this habit).

Mark told me that one of his top priorities is his family business.

Family is important. Business is important. I've got a great company, a great legacy, and my goal is to build on that and to nurture the next generation where possible to continue to invest in the business so that it continues to do well and prosper. So I put a lot of time into that. That is one of the things that I would like to have more time for, just for the succession planning and the work that goes around that, because it is work. If you just [say], "Well, we'll see what happens," that doesn't work out well.

You have got to manage the family process actively. Fortunately, there are a lot of resources out there that can help, because there are so many family businesses now. While they might be very different in terms of industry, there is a lot that they have in common. Whether they are large or small, 80 percent of the issues are pretty much the same. . . . It's important to know what these businesses look like and the typical traps they fall into. Because you've got not only the business issues, but you have the whole dynamic of family and all that that represents, so I have put some thought into that as well.

He also works hard to protect his family time at home.

A night at home doing nothing is a real luxury. I try to protect those times a little bit more than others. Otherwise, the evenings can be relatively full also.

Mark also prioritizes his workout time. Not only does he and his company sponsor and endorse a professional cycling team, he is also an avid cyclist.

Now, in biking weather, I do block a lot of time for that. There are groups that I ride with or certain events that I do. Whether it is the morning workout or an actual event, you've got to block the time, you know. It has to be as important as any other meeting. Nobody is going to give you that time if you do not take it for yourself. So I block those times and everybody knows that. They do not know the details. They just say I'm not here.

To drive this home, Mark also prioritizes working out, nutrition, and recovery to fuel his overall success as a CEO.

I probably average between six to seven hours of sleep; it is probably closer to six. I get up at six in the morning—I have a little workout routine. Nothing too much. Some stretching and Pilates-type stuff every morning. Two mornings a week I will do an hour of weight training. I have a small gym at home, which is perfect for that, and then depending on the season, my workout routine changes.

I eat a light breakfast, normally a coffee, eggs, and some grapefruit. I eat a reasonably light lunch and I usually have a pretty big dinner. I know that is not the normal program most people do, but I have always enjoyed cooking and eating good food. So for me, dinner is really important and I refuse to just have a pizza or have a sandwich unless I am really desperate. I would rather take the time and either go out or make a nice dinner. That is always part of my routine and I enjoy that. I usually have a couple glasses of wine with dinner. Not all the time, but more often than not. Never or very rarely during the day do I have anything to drink.

During the day my schedule is pretty full; I travel quite a bit for work, have meetings, spend time with customers, and of course keep up with e-mail. I just came back Sunday from a two-week trip in Asia and the Middle East. That throws off your schedule completely, and you're exercising less and you're eating more. During trips like that, I do now go crazy, because it is harder to recalibrate when I get back as I get older. My sleep is off. Everything takes longer. As you age, I think, even a good workout takes longer to recover from.

You may not know Greg Renker, but you have likely seen one of his commercials for beauty products (Proactiv+®, Meaningful Beauty,

WEN® Haircare). Greg is the founding principal and co-chairman of Guthy-Renker, one of the most successful and reputable direct marketing companies in the world. When I asked Greg who *he* would say he was, he answered: "father, husband, tennis and golf enthusiast, executive." It is pretty easy to see where his priorities lie: family, health, and then business.

I asked him more about how he fits in family, working out, and work on a regular basis. Here is a day in the life of Greg:

That's a great question. First of all, I fit it in because I'm blessed. I'm blessed to live in a country that enabled me to build my own business, so the free enterprise system and capitalism enable me to have the freedom to make that choice. Therefore, because I have my own business, I set my own schedule, including when I travel.

Yes, I'm in the gym every morning at seven a.m. and I leave the gym between eight thirty and nine. I'm always in the gym a minimum of ninety minutes, usually two hours. I always use a trainer unless I'm riding a bike. I never work out without a trainer. That's a pet peeve. I want to do the proper technique. I want someone else to do the thinking for me. I also enjoy being in the moment of working out . . . not anxious to get it over with and finished with it, but appreciating it while I'm doing it. The beauty of having a quality trainer is that it enables you to focus on the moment and the technique and the movement, so it becomes very precise and it's a lot like your favorite sport. It's like being totally into golf where you really, really want to get better each time you do it. You're trying to get better. That's what makes it fun.

Then I go to the office. I would say five days a week, I'm moving again by five thirty p.m., either on the tennis court, on a bike, or in a pool for a thirty-minute to forty-five-minute burst before dinner. That's the routine.

Patty Aubery is the president of Jack Canfield Companies, the umbrella organization that oversees the training, events, and coaching practice of Jack Canfield, author of the popular *Chicken Soup for the Soul* series. She names health as one of her top priorities.

I think health is a huge component of the different areas in your life. You know, we talk about business and health and home and relationships and everything else. I joke about it: I say, "If I'm sad, everybody's miserable." When you don't feel good, you don't have the clarity you need. You don't have the stamina you need. You don't have the sleep that you need. I mean, everything's kind of off. And I also believe that it's something we can completely control in our lives. It's a formula, like everything else—just like success. And I tell people [when] they say "How much do you weigh?" [that] I don't weigh myself, because I know if I'm doing the right things I don't need to. I'll be a size four. It's just clear.

Jerry Oshinsky, the attorney known as "the father of insurance law," views family as his top priority.

Well, I think family always comes first over everything else. I've always been very fortunate in being very fast at what I do and being able to absorb a lot of information in a hurry. Fortunately for me, I don't have to worry about any of the things that most people worry about, [such as] where do you write your checks, and where is your bank account, and how do you pay the mortgage? My wife, Sandy, does all of that. I have no idea how any of that works, and I've never had to do any of that. She even prints my boarding passes for the trips. I've been very fortunate in having that kind of support. . . . I can focus on the substance of the legal work that I do and also spend a lot of time with the family and [at] family events like soccer games and basketball games and tennis matches and things like that.

Plus, I've never needed a lot of sleep. I've always been able to get by most of the time on five or six hours. Every so often I have to catch up, but I've usually been able to spend eighteen hours a day doing things, which allows me to spend time not only on my professional life but also my personal life.

Set Boundaries

Once you've set your top priorities, your next task in creating your routine is *setting boundaries* around those priorities. Patty notes that women in particular tend to feel guilty about setting boundaries around time:

I think the biggest struggles really come from your belief about time and where you should spend it. I think a lot of women spend time feeling guilty. They feel guilty when they're not at work, and they feel guilty when they're not at home. And so for me, it's more about living in the moment and being present wherever I am.

The ability to be present in the moment is a sign you've not only set clear priorities, but that you've set clear boundaries around your priorities; you know that what you're doing right now is exactly what you need to be doing. Also, when you focus on being present in the moment, fully aware of your surroundings, you can also make good decisions about new requests. Instead of saying yes to a request without thinking, you can take a second to remember what is truly important to you and choose what would produce a positive result in your life.

Before I got married and started a family, for many years I used to work twelve to fourteen hours a day, five to seven days a week. Truthfully, I had no boundaries regarding my work time because at that point in my life, I had no competing priorities. My choice was simple: More work equals more money, so work more hours.

Since I've gotten married, I have learned to set boundaries because I have new priorities: I love to spend time with my wife and enjoy fun activities with her. I simply make a choice: I choose to spend time with my wife rather than work ridiculously long hours. When I became a father, my boundaries became even more sacred to me. Family time definitely trumps working too many hours, and when I am careful to maintain the boundaries between work time and family time, I am simultaneously creating a higher demand for my work time. It's simply a fallacy now that more work equals more money. The opposite is actually true: Less work equals more money, because my rates have increased due to demand.

So setting boundaries all comes down to making a choice. In every scenario, we always have the choice to say yes or no to an opportunity or request, and this choice can lead to either negative or positive circumstances for us. We may not always like our choices, but the choice is always ours. Uber successful people understand this: They are fully present in the moment and aware of their surroundings, and they make choices to set appropriate boundaries on their time according to the situation. Angel Martinez is the CEO, president, and board chair of Deckers Outdoor Corporation, a footwear manufacturer with seven popular brands including Teva, UGG Australia, Sanuk, and Hoka One One. Angel understands the power of choice in creating necessary boundaries (with the help of his wife, he admits). In his company, he tries to help his employees set healthy boundaries as well.

We hire a lot of people (we have quite a few employees now), and I'm looking for balanced employees. I'm looking for balanced people. People who don't live in an office and just never leave the office. I want people to get out and do stuff on the weekends, during the week, at lunch time, whenever. Our team tries to facilitate that.

As a matter of fact, our new office building is going to have a workout facility, a third-of-a-mile jogging path around a marsh area, basketball courts, and other fun stuff. In addition, we've also included a program for smoking cessation, weight loss, and a variety of other things.

First things first, you've got to be a healthy person. That's all part of being a productive employee. If you're not, I don't believe you're going to be that productive, and I think you're going to be very unhappy. Plus, it's not good for the culture in the company if people are stressed out, unhappy, and feeling trapped by work.

Setting boundaries on your time, so you can honor your commitments and know when it's time to shift to your next priority, helps keep you balanced and healthy.

Get Up Early

Because we now live in a world with 24/7 instant access and communication, even when we clearly set our priorities it can still be difficult to fit everything into a day. This is why my most successful clients find it extremely important to wake up early.

Jim Corcoran is senior vice president of Morgan Stanley Wealth Management. He's clear about his family priorities and wants to be a good example for his kids, and for him, it all comes down to getting up early.

You get your ass up early in the morning. What else do you want me to say? After work, my kids have games and I want to be there. They are all active, and the reason they are active is because they see

*me being active and I'm in their face encouraging them, but they
are talented as well. They see me working, they know how fit I am,
and they are saying, "Hey, I can be as healthy as that."*

I know, I know, a lot people say they are "night owls" and just "can't"
get up early. But I believe it also comes down to making a choice in light
of what you really want in life. So here are ten reasons why getting out
of bed sooner so often leads to success.

1. **Set a Relaxed Pace:** Early rising sets off a chain reaction that's
   favorable to you. You can prepare for work earlier, and you
   have more time throughout the day to work out, think, and
   tackle projects or chores. Then, when evening rolls around,
   you can relax.
2. **Sit in Less Traffic:** If you wake up early enough, you can drive
   to work before the roadways are clogged, which means less
   daily stress.
3. **Catch Up on Reading:** With extra time in the morning, you
   might survey your favorite media outlets and get caught up
   with the latest news and sports. That way, you'll have plenty of
   conversation starters throughout the day.
4. **Get Organized**: Instead of rushing out the door, you'll be able
   to take your time collecting your materials, planning activities
   for the day, and responding to e-mails.
5. **Eat Bigger Breakfasts:** When you consume a substantial,
   balanced breakfast, you supply your body and your brain with
   the nutrients they require to perform at peak levels.
6. **Fit in Your Morning Workout:** Morning exercise wakes up
   your mind and prepares your muscles to burn as many calories
   as possible throughout the day.

7. **Experience Dawn:** Witnessing a sunrise is magical; at dawn the world takes on a transcendent glow. It's enough to put you in a good mood for quite some time.

8. **Emulate the Greats:** Many successful people over the centuries have been early birds, from Ben Franklin to Barack Obama, and from Virgin founder Richard Branson to Disney CEO Bob Iger.

9. **Do Something New:** You can use the time you would have spent under the sheets trying out a new activity—something to sharpen your mind, your body, or both. Go for walks. Complete crossword puzzles. Build birdhouses. The possibilities are endless.

10. **Be Forceful:** Instead of dreading mornings and getting up at the last possible moment, take control. Prove to yourself that you have the power and the discipline to rise early, that you embrace the world rather than shrink from it. You might be amazed at how this attitude can spill over into other areas of your life.

So the first healthy habit for success is to *create a routine* by setting priorities, setting boundaries, and getting up early. In the next chapter, we'll learn about the second healthy habit for success: how to grow your career from your passion.

Chapter 2
GROW YOUR CAREER FROM YOUR PASSION

If you want to be successful at work, it helps if you love what you do. Passion for your work gives you the resilience to face daily setbacks and eventually beat the odds that are stacked against you. It causes you to seek out new opportunities that pass other people by. Even if you never make a lot of money, being able to do what you love every day is its own form of success and wealth.

All of the people I interviewed are passionate, and they have all found a way to connect their passion and their work in some way. No two stories are the same, but they each have something important to teach us about the importance of passion in our work.

Passion Creates and Attracts Opportunity

Under Angel Martinez's leadership as CEO, Deckers has grown from $200 million in revenue to over $1.6 billion. But Angel didn't begin his career with a goal to be the CEO of Deckers; he began with a passion for running. To understand how his passion led to his success, Angel takes us back more than thirty-five years:

> *In college I was a competitive runner, and I just realized at some point in the middle of my college career that I wanted to make a living from my passion, which was running. At the time, the running boom was really in full cycle. I saw a lot of people I knew were making a living in the running business. I figured if they could do it, I could do it.*
>
> *A bunch of these guys I used to run against were working for this funky little startup company in Beaverton, Oregon, called Nike. So I decided I was going to open a running shoe store. There weren't very many running shoe specialty stores at that time. As a matter of fact, the store I opened was really the first one in the country. It was called Starting Line Sports, in Mountain View, California.*

Notice that Angel began with a passion for running and then made a conscious decision to find a way to make money with that passion. As a runner himself in the midst of the running boom, he saw an opportunity that others couldn't see, and he opened the first running store in the country to cater to this growing sport. His passion created an opportunity where none existed before. He goes on to explain:

> *I had a partnership with Runner's World magazine at the time. I sold their books and the magazines and all the stuff that went with it. I had access to their mail-order list, which at the time was 350,000, and we sold mail-order running products. In*

those days, running shoes were hard to get. We also introduced Casio stopwatches to America and first introduced Gore-Tex in running suits.

After about three years, I had two stores. Then three years after that I met a guy who was trying to bring a brand over from England called Reebok. I was familiar with Reebok because I had worn it in high school. I met this guy. One thing led to another, and I was the third employee hired. I still kept my stores, but now I was also repping for Reebok. I had Northern California, Oregon, and Washington as my territories. I was also doing the product marketing for Reebok as well, so I was wearing multiple hats.

Although Angel could have stopped at being a store owner, his passion for running and his experience selling running products attracted a new opportunity to represent Reebok.

I eventually sold my stores. I was with Reebok for twenty-one years and became its chief marketing officer. We bought the Rockport Company, which is another shoe brand, and I ran that company for five years as CEO. When I left Reebok in 2001 to take some time off and basically retire, I got bored after a little while and started teaching track and cross country at my son's high school.

Then we started up another brand called Keen Footwear, which makes toe-protection sandals. That went pretty well. During that time my wife and I bought property in Santa Barbara, and we made the move. I met the CEO and founder of Deckers. He had been wanting to get out for years and had been looking for his replacement. I sort of showed up in town, and he recruited me. I sold my interest in Keen and joined Deckers. We were doing about $200 million at the time in revenue. Now we're doing $1.6 billion. We've grown a bit.

From Reebok to Rockport, we see again how his passion continued to attract opportunity. But when Angel was teaching track in retirement, he certainly didn't have to start a new footwear brand. That is just what passion does: Not only does it attract opportunity, it creates it. It should not surprise us that now, as the CEO of Deckers, Angel is passionate about passionate employees, but we will get to that in a later chapter.

Passion Beats the Odds

Ema Boateng is a professional soccer player from Ghana currently playing for the Swedish football club in Helsingborg. He grew up in a home with no running water or electricity, but today he plays on the world stage of professional soccer. Here is the story of how he found his passion, which led him to beat all the odds.

> *Learning to play in Ghana was different than here in the United States—it's tough. I was lucky enough to have shoes. Not everyone had shoes. Sometimes we would have a good grass field, but most of the time we played on dirt. And if we didn't have a field, we would just play anywhere. I have so many cuts on my knees from just playing on the road; we would put cones on the road and start playing. If a car came by, we stopped and let the car pass, and then we would go back to it. Soccer was our lives and it was all we knew; everyone just wanted to play.*

The soccer culture in Ghana formed a genuine passion in Ema. No obstacle, no circumstance, no lack, and no excuse stood between his friends and the thrill of a game. His passion was rewarded with an opportunity when, at fifteen years old, he was awarded a scholarship from the Right to Dream Academy to go to Cate School in Carpintiera, California, where he could continue high school and play soccer.

My dad really supported me and wanted me to play. To some extent it was because he wanted me to go to school and focus on education, and he knew soccer would help me get there. He loved it as much as I did; he played it too!

Ema's father's passion for soccer and greater vision for what soccer could do for Ema helped him navigate the opportunities before him. He even surprised himself:

I never really thought I would come to the United States and go through this way and still have love for [the game]. This has been the best experience, getting to live here and learn how things work, instead of staying in Ghana until I was eighteen and jumping to professional soccer right away. I think this way is the best.

In 2012, he received the annual Gatorade Player of the Year award. He finished high school early and began college at the University of California, Santa Barbara. During the summer of 2013, he was invited by Helsingborg to train with them and was later offered a contract.

Ema fulfilled the dream so many young athletes have to play their sport professionally. He beat all the odds and found a way to connect his passion and his profession. But how did someone who started with so little rise to such great heights? Desire, raw talent, and the right opportunities were certainly factors, but many aspiring athletes have had these and more. I think the answer lies in the fact that Ema pursued all of the opportunities before him with the same passion he had when he would let nothing stand between him and a good game of soccer with his friends.

Passion Seeks Excellence

As founding principal and co-chairman of direct marketing company Guthy-Renker, Greg Renker has a passion for advertising. But how did he get that passion and what can we learn from it?

> *In college, I didn't have any money, and I had to pay my own way. I recognized that the only way to really achieve my goals was to learn how to be a salesman. I knew I wanted to start my own business, and I felt like being a salesman was just like having your own business, because you're totally responsible for the output and you get to drive the results, assuming you're passionate about the product. So I began selling outdoor advertising in college and discovered that I loved advertising.*

Notice that unlike Angel Martinez and Ema Boateng, Greg did not necessarily start out knowing his passion; he started with the need to make enough money to put himself through college. We all face responsibilities we can't avoid, but those responsibilities don't have to be obstacles to finding our true passion. They may be exactly what we needed to discover it. Greg is a good example of someone who discovered his passion along the way.

> *The combination of wanting to be a really good salesman, plus loving advertising, led me to the industry that I am in now. In the mid-eighties I saw these television pitch people selling no-down-payment real estate courses on TV. It was all kind of schlocky—carnival sales—and I knew that I could do it better. That's how I teamed up with Bill Guthy, who had the exact same idea at the*

same time. But we still needed a product and to understand how it's all getting done. That's what led us to start Guthy-Renker.

He saw that television advertising was effective but also knew it could be taken to the next level. And after Guthy-Renker elevated their own game, they helped the industry as a whole raise the bar by establishing professional standards for advertising by cofounding the Electronic Retailing Association. Greg's passion for advertising drove him to seek excellence in an industry that was not always known for excellence, and it led directly to his success in that industry.

When you find your passion and build your career around that passion, many of the components of success fall naturally into place. Angel Martinez's career showed us how passion opens our eyes to new opportunities that would otherwise pass us by—both in the form of opportunities that we create and opportunities that we attract to ourselves. Despite tremendous effort, Ema Boateng's passion made his path through economic obstacles and tremendous odds seem almost natural. Greg Renker's career in the advertising industry shows us how passion for your work results in the desire to seek excellence. Opportunity, resilience, and excellence are not only the byproducts of passion, they are also key components of success and wealth, however you define it.

One quick word of encouragement if you have not yet found your true passion in life: Although Angel and Ema discovered their passion at an early age, Greg discovered it in college, and some discover it even later in life. The key is to keep moving forward, pay attention, and move toward those things you naturally enjoy and have a passion for.

Chapter 3
COLLABORATE

When we think of collaboration, we might think of any number of contexts, such as teamwork, leadership, acknowledging effort, and even liking and sharing social media posts.

At its very heart, collaboration is people working together toward a common goal. It is the synergy of ideas. It is combined effort. It is facing problems together and implementing solutions. It is the shared experience of victory and defeat. It might even be leaving it all behind over a drink after work.

Everyone that I interviewed is phenomenal at collaborating with others, and they credit their success to those who helped them along the way. Many have created entire companies around a culture of creativity and collaboration.

They taught me that who you choose to collaborate with, how well you collaborate, and your ability to facilitate the collaboration of others will to a large extent determine your success both financially and in terms of satisfaction with your life. Greg Renker puts it this way:

The people we choose to spend time with have a very powerful influence on our actions, on our perceptions, and also on our motivations. So if you can get control over your thoughts, number one, and then number two, [determine how to] use those thoughts in association with others, I would say you are 75 percent of the way toward achieving your goal.

To break down this huge topic and make it actionable, we are going to cover three critical aspects of collaboration: building your own personal support system, surrounding yourself with the perfect team at work, and valuing your team.

Build Your Personal Support System

As Greg Renker said, the people you choose to spend time with will have an immense influence over you, so it is critical that you intentionally surround yourself with people who will help you get to where you want to go. A personal support system goes far beyond our work life. A personal support system includes all the people that shape your life direction: the mentors you admire and seek advice from, the professionals you hire to help you overcome a problem, and the people you live with at home.

Mentors

Patty Aubery, president of Jack Canfield Companies, began scheduling for Jack even before his book was successful, and she has risen to the top of the organization to manage the day-to-day affairs of Jack's companies. Patty says,

> *If you're new in business, it's critical to have the right counsel and people around you: mentors.*

Very successful people, like Patty, had and still have very successful mentors. No matter where you are on your journey, there is almost always someone who has gone farther, done more, and already knows what you need to learn to take the next step. Mentors can keep you focused amid distractions. They point the way when you come to a crucial crossroads. And sometimes they can even open doors for you. Your mentor can be someone in your organization but often is someone in your industry or an adjacent industry you admire and who is willing to collaborate with you and help shape your life and career.

Professionals You Hire

While a mentor is a generalist who can help you with the big picture, the professionals you hire to help you with a particular issue are the specialists, such as a lawyer, an accountant, or even a business coach.

As a personal trainer, I am just one example of this kind of professional who plays a focused role in someone's personal support system. I have helped athletes overcome a particular injury or get to the next level physically. I also have helped other professionals (like the people in this book) who understand how their fitness is critical to their overall success and want to maximize the effectiveness of the time they spend training. I know firsthand how a professional can shorten the learning curve in developing new skills, and I help people avoid costly mistakes. I allow people to focus on what they are doing without having to worry about whether they are doing it right—and as a result, they get a lot more out of their workouts. In addition to working one on one with individuals, I also help companies implement effective wellness programs that improve productivity and company culture.

Think about the areas of your life that could benefit from focused training or professional advice. It could be anything from nutrition to finances. Successful people know they don't have time to figure everything out for themselves. They collaborate with trusted advisors. It may cost you some money in the short term, but in the long term it will save you much more in time, mistakes avoided, and peace of mind.

Family

Another critical aspect of your personal support system is your family—most importantly, your life partner. When you get married, you are making a lifelong commitment to someone else, so you need to be on the same page regarding family growth, schedules, balance, routine, and passion. Here is what Angel Martinez has to say about this:

> *My wife and I made an agreement a long time [ago]—she's fitness oriented too—both of us just felt it was important for the kids to have healthy parents. That's always been a priority. Neither of us has ever complained when the other one's got to go work out for a while. We take turns. It's just always been part of the deal. As a matter of fact, if I go a few days without working out, she starts bugging me. "You've got to go work out . . . you haven't worked out!" I think she senses the stress building up, and she wants me to manage that. She's always been a big factor. I think it's important upfront to have an agreement about what role fitness plays in your life with your partner. If you can't agree on that, you may have the wrong partner.*

Of course as a trainer, I couldn't agree more with what Angel has to say about fitness, but his point is much bigger than that. Angel had an important goal, and he couldn't have managed it without the support of his wife. In turn, he supported her goals. Your family can be a huge encouragement through stressful and difficult times, but they can also add stress and difficulty. The key is to have alignment and support in all of the major areas that matter to all of you.

Ema Boateng's story is a good example of how a great personal support system can pull all of the moving parts of life together and make overcoming obstacles and navigating difficult decisions look easy to the outside world. His coaches, the staff, his family in Ghana, and his host family in the United States all collaborated to help him make the transition from living in Ghana to living in the United States, from high school to college, and then ultimately to professional soccer. Here he describes the support in his own words:

I've got a lot of people supporting me: my host family here in the United States, Mark and Linda; Tom from the Right to Dream Academy; my parents; and you, Perry. It's been good learning and getting experience from these people. I can't thank these people enough, especially Mark and Linda. They have made my last four years incredible. The relationship is deep—not just with them, but with their family too. They have just been there for me every time, for anything I need. As I'm talking right now, Mark is working on my passport and trying to get my visa for upcoming trips.

Whether I am at their house or at the academy in Ghana, I just feel [at] home. We keep in contact; they are still trying to shape things for me in the future by talking to teams about my progress. I talk to Mark and Linda all the time. I talk to my family too—they encourage me to just do what I want to do as long as it is safe.

Before my junior year of high school, I wanted to go play pro right away. I talked to Mark, Tom, and my parents about everything. Even though we discussed it over the course of many years, I was still hesitant. I wanted to play right away, and they all advised [me] to give myself a lot more options—so that's how I ended up in college. I have learned a lot this year, and I think it was a good decision to collaborate with them and take their advice.

As a young person overwhelmed with new opportunities, Ema needed every aspect of his personal support system to help him stay focused and make the right decisions. Whether you are a young athlete, new to the business world, or are just taking the next big step in your life or career, the feeling of being overwhelmed is the same. We are all prone to shortsightedness and lack of confidence in those situations. Intentionally surrounding yourself with the right mentors, professionals, and home life can really make or break you.

Surround Yourself with the "Perfect" Team

The next practical aspect of collaboration I learned from my clients is to surround yourself with the perfect team at work. Of course, by "perfect" I don't really mean perfect. I mean perfect *for you.* Just as your personal support system can make or break your major life decisions, the people you surround yourself with at work can make or break you there. As Patty Aubery says,

Surround yourself with the perfect people. If you can find those people who really support you in the areas you're not as strong in, you'll be even more successful.

Michael Fitzpatrick, former CEO of PacTel, agrees with Patty, and reminds us that we don't need to view our weaknesses negatively, but as positive opportunities for improvement and collaboration:

The mistake that many people make is they refuse to recognize that they have areas for improvement—and to me it's not a weakness, it's an area for improvement. You just need a lot more improvement in that area than you do in some others. In the case of work, for example, I try to hire people who have a real positive skill in that area that's not as strong for me. That's the really key thing: Surround yourself with people who are the very best in the areas that are not your strong points.

No one is good at everything, so you have to find people who are good at the things you aren't good at and learn to collaborate with them. It's true of the people you choose to work with, like business associates and partners, and it's also true of the people you choose to hire as employees.

Business Associates and Partners

Before you accept a new position at a new company, take a good look around at the people you will be working with every day, because they will have a profound impact on where you go and how you feel about getting there. It's even more true if you go into business with a partner. Greg Renker considers partnering with Bill Guthy to be one of the most pivotal opportunities in his life. He describes it this way:

So that was the number-one best decision: having an amazing partner who I'm still with twenty-five years later. We both had the exact same idea at the same time—it was a perfect match.

That's what we call a mastermind. It's usually a group of brains solving problems. That's very rewarding. You don't actually ever feel quite alone when you have partnerships and a team.

If you pick the perfect team, problems and obstacles are just opportunities for collaboration, problem solving, synergy, and momentum. If you pick the wrong team, problems are opportunities for arguments, turf wars, and a dead-end career. Make sure you pick a winning team.

Employees

Hiring employees is another opportunity to find strengths to complement your weaknesses. However, credentials and skill sets are not the only thing to look for in new employees, as Mark Bissell has learned:

> *Having a good team of people is so important. However, even more critical is having loyal people working with you. College credentials can be important, but I have noticed that they don't necessarily translate to success. You can have really smart people, but if they are disruptive or they don't know how to get things done, they are just not going to be successful. I have learned through trial and error that an employee's alignment with the company's culture is critical.*
>
> *Opportunity costs, hiring the wrong people, and wasting time are the biggest costs to me. Those are years that you never get back. I wish I had understood that a little bit better and put more time into organizational development earlier in my career.*

An employee's ability to collaborate with you and with others may be just as important as the particular skills that they bring to the table. Notice that Mark measures the cost of mistakes in this area in years, not weeks or months. Your job as a leader is not only to pick the right team, but also to facilitate the collaboration of the team. Help create the mastermind experience that Greg Renker talked about among your employees.

Value Your Team

The final practical aspect of collaboration I learned from my clients is to value your team. Everyone wants to feel appreciated and feel like they are making a valuable contribution. A close friend of mine, Brian, is a CEO of a local company. He has created a vibrant company culture because he knows that growing employees in a great work environment helps sell more software. He is one of those leaders who has a natural ability to make everyone feel important. He explains that sometimes the little things, like remembering everyone's name or making a big deal about introducing the new hires to the company, pay big dividends in terms of making sure his employees are thriving on a daily basis, not just surviving. For example, to acknowledge people's efforts, Brian created an incredibly popular incentive program around a simple T-shirt. Monthly, his company gives a "shout-out" T-shirt and special parking spot to an employee they feel has gone above and beyond.

Jerry Oshinsky shared a great story about the value of acknowledging everyone on your team.

> Years ago we had what I like to call a "beauty contest," where [clients] interview different law firms to see who they want to hire. I decided to bring in the entire team, including the legal assistant, who was a very sparkling woman. We went around the room, and I said to the client, "I'd like you to hear from each one of our folks, and they will tell you a little bit about themselves and what they do." We went around the room. We had everybody. There were about five or six of us in the room—lawyers, partners, associates, and the legal assistant. After the meeting, the client hired us, and they told me that one of the principal reasons we got retained was they'd never been in a beauty contest before where the attorneys brought in their legal assistant and had her explain what she did.

He went on to explain that the legal assistant does all the grunt work and knows where everything is, down to the last scrap of paper. Giving her a voice and acknowledging her significance not only made her day, but also won the trust of a new client.

To come full circle, one of the most important ways you can value your team is to add value to them in the form of mentoring and career development. Mark Bissell explains,

Take the time to bring young people along through mentoring, continuing education, additional experience, and exposure, because that is the future of the company. Sometimes you have to hire people from the outside to get a certain skill set; just recognize that you are going to be more sustainable if you can promote from within and do your own in-house development.

Concerning mentoring, Jerry Oshinsky says,

I've always believed very firmly that the people who work with me should also be successful in their own way and create their own successful career paths. There have been a lot of people in my life I've worked with who have branched out and become tremendously successful on their own.

Because mentors are so critical to helping you find your own path, take the time to be a critical part of someone else's career path, even if it leads them somewhere else. Mark Bissell shows us that it's just good business, and Jerry Oshinsky shows us that it's good to be proud of the success of others.

With a couple of exceptions, I have had the opportunity to meet all of the clients interviewed in this book because at some point they invited me to be a part of their personal support system as a trainer. I have had the privilege to learn from great leaders who were great team builders and who knew how to value those teams. Most of all, they have taught me that collaboration is not just a skill or a means to an end, but that it is a way of life.

Chapter 4
LEARN FROM YOUR MISTAKES

I know, I know—no one enjoys making mistakes. But the truth is we're all going to make mistakes from time to time, no matter how successful we've been in the past. The most successful people know how to turn their mistakes to their advantage because they view them first and foremost as opportunities to learn.

The Cost of Doing Business

We failed often, because the way our business worked was that we would make bets on products and product ideas. Then we would develop a production to try to sell these products via thirty minutes on television. We never knew upfront whether or not we were going to succeed, whether or not the decision we were making was going to be a good one, so we failed all the time. We had many, many experiences where after one year or two years of developmental work on a project, which ultimately became a thirty-minute infomercial, we would put it on television and not get any orders. Consumers just simply didn't respond.

We went through a period in which one or two winners could pay for six or seven losers. All those failures, though, taught us so much. The real value in what we know now and the reason we're still working hard at our company is that our failures taught us things our competitors will never know. Our competitors come in and make mistakes we were making fifteen years ago. We're very blessed that we made it through the failures and handled the financial reversals associated with them because it's only made us a better and more prosperous company now.

Reflecting on Greg Renker's story above, in the rapidly growing TV advertising business, failure was simply the cost of doing business. Failure was the price of learning, and learning from those mistakes was the key to success.

However, failure is not the only way to learn from mistakes. Greg goes on to say,

When we started in the business, I was very competitive and very curious about what my competitors were doing. I used every piece of intelligence I could. I asked a lot of people a lot of questions about what my competitors were doing and how they were doing it.

If I saw a competitor [was] successful, I tried to understand exactly what map they used to get there. In many ways, our company was modeled starting twenty years ago after our number-one competitor, so there was a company that was doing what we

wanted to do. They were doing it effectively and admirably. We looked at that model and said, "That's the one that we're going to mimic, but we can do it better," and we did. We did it better and we did it more aggressively, but if it hadn't been for competition, we actually would not have known exactly what to do.

Learning from your own mistakes is great, but learning from the mistakes of others is even better. Greg imitated the success of his competitors because there was no need to go back and make the same mistakes they did. That gave him more time to make mistakes of his own, taking the same ideas to the next level. You don't have to stub your toe on every rock along the path or reinvent the wheel. Becoming a student of the success of others and the inevitable failures that led them there can help you navigate the road ahead much more smoothly.

The Smartest Decision Isn't Always the Best Decision

When I asked Jerry Oshinsky what he had learned from his mistakes, this is what he said:

As a young and developing attorney, I think you get so wrapped up in the legal theories and cases you're arguing that you sometimes forget, at the end of the day, it's the client's interest that counts. The client doesn't care how good your memory is, how smart you are, or how well you present a case—the client cares about the result. The client also cares about what it's going to cost to get there. You have to balance the result with the cost of getting the result.

Today, we're very sensitive to making sure that if we're going to do something in a case, number one, we always run it past the client first. Lots of lawyers in this world don't understand this, especially small-town lawyers who represent clients on small cases— they just go ahead and do things. We never do anything in a case without checking with the clients first and saying, "Here's what we're thinking about, here's what we'd like to do, and here's what we think it's going to cost to get there."

Most of our clients are large entities—corporations, universities, municipal entities—who have their own attorneys, so we usually deal with an attorney inside the organization. We also run everything past that person. I think from a stake standpoint, that's not something I really understood as a young attorney or something I learned growing up. As a young lawyer I spent a lot of time and effort getting to results that probably cost more than it was worth to the client. It was great from my standpoint intellectually, but it wasn't what the client was expecting.

What Jerry learned over the course of his career is bigger than a single lesson from a single mistake or even a series of mistakes. It raises the fundamental question of what counts as success, and what counts as failure. In any business context, you can succeed by your own standards but fail by the standards of others. This is not an easy lesson to learn, because you have to step outside of yourself and be willing to see things from another's perspective. Learning this lesson allowed Jerry to learn from mistakes that many of his colleagues couldn't even see, and it took his career to a whole new level of effectiveness because he served his clients on their own terms.

Pace Yourself

I decided that this chapter on mistakes is a good opportunity for me to share some of my own story, because I have certainly made my fair share of mistakes.

When I was sixteen years old and in high school, my goal was to play professional football. I became obsessed with working out, and over the next two years, I went from 185 to 255 pounds. I learned how to eat a lot of healthy food to gain good weight, plus I learned all of the proper Olympic lifting methods to build strength. But I hurt my back multiple times in the process, and I eventually had to give up that dream of playing professional football.

Knowing my future had changed, I wanted to shed the seventy pounds I had gained. So . . . what did I do? I decided I wanted to run a marathon before I went to college the following year. I ran too much, ate too little, never stretched, lacked proper coaching, and basically became anorexic and endurance crazed. If you have ever bonked on a long training run or ride, or overtrained for a race, you know that feeling—it sucks. However, eight months of not training properly did teach me how to train properly for the next marathon.

The next mistake happened to be part of my first Ironman Triathlon during my first year of college. I was already interning at a physical therapy office and mentoring under Peter Park, one of the best personal trainers in the world. I knew that I was going to fail many times in the process of trying to complete an Ironman; however, I was confident that failure would ultimately lead to success because I had arranged for the proper support. I had Peter coaching me, proper gear, hundreds of training hours under my belt—yet I still made tons of mistakes.

I was twenty years old at the time, and mentally I was too young to do a race of this caliber. Once again, I overtrained, overscheduled myself with work and school, and got way too caught up in trying to go fast and be competitive. I remember the day of the triathlon like it was yesterday. I was obsessed with completing the race in under 10.5 hours, which meant I would have to swim 2.4 miles in under 1.25 hours, ride 112 miles in under 5.5 hours, and then run a marathon in under 3.5 hours—no matter what! It didn't matter that there were crosswinds that day in excess of 30 miles per hour.

All my heart rate training went out the window. I didn't care about the wind slowing me down; I was going to come in on the bike in under

5.5 hours at all costs. This led me to completely bonking in the first 6 miles of my run! I pretty much walked and half-jogged the remaining 20 miles (it hurt). My perfect race became the longest 12 hours of my life!

I was so overscheduled that I didn't even stop to reflect on the accomplishment of completing an Ironman in under 14 months of training at 20 years old. Instead, I threw my bike in my car, drove straight back to Santa Barbara from Arizona, and started work at five a.m. the next day, which included running and riding with my clients. Two weeks later, I raced in a half-Ironman completely overtrained and underrested.

I did everything I now coach others *not* to do, but I also learned firsthand how it feels to overtrain and fail. Fortunately I have also learned firsthand how it feels to train properly and succeed. Not only did I learn from my own mistakes as a competitive athlete, I prepared myself to be a better trainer. Wherever my clients are in the process, I know how they feel. My job as a trainer is to help them overcome their failures, learn from their mistakes, and ultimately be successful.

Failure Depends on Your Perspective

When I asked Kevin Haley, Under Armour's senior vice president of innovation, what he had learned from his own weaknesses and failures, his perspective surprised me.

> *Many people look at weakness and failure in a very binary way. It's either a weakness or it's a strength. It's either a success or a failure. I completely disagree with that point of view. I think oftentimes you will find that a perceived weakness or a failure can become a huge strength.*
>
> *For instance, the truck I'm driving in right now looks like a homeless person lives in it because there's so much crap in it. But, you know, having a tolerance for a certain level of what other people*

perceive as chaos allows me to juggle a lot of different things and feel comfortable with it. I have a lot of different balls up in the air. And some of those balls are going to turn into home runs and some of those balls are going to turn into strikeouts, and I'm okay with that. Because there are so many balls in the air, we'll be okay in the end.

That's a very different mentality than some people have. And that's okay. It works for me and it works for [my family]. At some level, it's who I am. I'm the fifth of six children. I married a woman who was one of six children. My dad was one of seven children. I have six children myself. So I live and know chaos. You can't keep everything straight with all of those different people. You just have to trust that things work themselves out. Everybody pitches in, everybody helps, and there's a little bit of team mentality.

And so, anyway, along with my idea of failure and weakness is just really being comfortable with a lot of disorder. Weakness and failures can be positive things. Somebody from the outside would say, "Kevin, you're so disorganized," or "You don't know how to focus," or "You have ADD"—all of which are true and can be negative. The key for me is to make a choice and to look at [my tolerance for chaos] as an enormous strength and an asset. Otherwise, if I try to keep that out of myself—become a CFO at an insurance company or something like that—I would be miserable. In fact, I was! I was an attorney in a law firm and I was miserable, but I convinced myself that I wasn't taking my job home with me. I told myself, "I'm not defined by what I do; I'm defined by who I am. I can do any job and be happy, and I'll have a positive outlook."

And [after] four years of telling myself that, my wife said, "You're lying to yourself, you are bringing it home, you're miserable, so you've got to get a new job." So I did by finding a job that requires and even rewards a little bit of chaos and disorder, and a little bit of ADD.

I have always imagined it this way: If I were blind, my hearing would become really good. My weakness has created strength in other areas.

I get to use all of my experience, including my marketing experience and consumer insight experience, to say what's best for our company. In a weird way, in a very circuitous path, it's all worked out. So, everything I've done in my whole life, good and bad, has prepared me for this job, which is a great feeling—plus a lot of fun.

Kevin teaches us that success and failure are a matter of perspective, and that what might be a failure in one context may be a success in another. In his case, failure would have been to stay in the same place and try to be someone he wasn't. Mistakes or failure in one context can help us find success in the next.

Like I said at the beginning of the chapter, success and failure are not opposites as long as you learn from your mistakes. Greg Renker showed us how, in the context of advertising, failure is just the price of doing business. Jerry Oshinsky taught us to be mindful of our client's definition of success. On the other hand, Kevin Haley reminded us that sometimes we need to take a step back and make sure we are a good fit for a particular context. Don't just learn from your mistakes in the past; expect to learn from your mistakes in the future. Don't be afraid to fail!

Chapter 5
LEAD FROM WITHIN

B eing a leader is hard work. For some people, leadership comes naturally, and for others it is a learned art. Whether it comes naturally or not, great leadership comes from a deep well of inner strength combined with dreams, vision, self-awareness, and the ability to face fears. Leaders are not just CEO's of Fortune 500 companies. Be a leader to your daughter, an exceptional co-worker, or community leader and when the opportunity presents itself, be brave and step forward with leadership on your success path. This chapter explores these themes of leadership and the inner life through the reflections of great leaders.

Lead Yourself

Great leaders are able to lead themselves. You have to have the inner strength to define yourself, and not let other people or circumstances define you. Will Chesebro is someone I admire precisely because of this kind of inner strength. He was born with cerebral palsy on his left side, but that didn't keep him from going to the world championships for para-cycling in 2011 and 2012. He keeps a grueling training schedule where, in his own words, he is always on the thin line between high performance and injury. Listen to him talk about what it is like to chart your own course in life with a disability.

You can't worry about how other people view you. I would say the biggest thing is that I was born with the disability. I didn't have an accident. I didn't get ill. I wasn't injured in war. I was born with a disability that is very evident. I am not missing any limbs, but I limp every single day of my life, and people, when they first see me, wonder what's wrong with me. I've had issues in school and in life, but it's how you conduct yourself on a daily basis that leads to your success. I never let my disability define me as a person. My work ethic, my results, and how I treat other people . . . that what's defines me . . . my disability doesn't define me. My disability is only physical, it's not mental, so I'm very capable of anything I do. The main thing is to live the life that you want to live and not let other people tell you that there is something that you can't do, because if you try hard enough, and you sacrifice enough, you can do whatever you want.

Some of life's challenges are within, and some come from external circumstances; however, all of us could use some of Will's grit to face the challenges ahead.

Dream Big

Great leaders dream big. According to Michael Fitzpatrick, tech entrepreneur and former CEO of PacTel,

> *You have to have dreams, and you have to think big. Many people don't dream big enough, and even if you don't achieve that dream, you're going to achieve a much higher level of success than you would have if you'd set your goals too low. This is true for both business and sports—you have to dream big.*
>
> *If you want to be an average golfer or tennis player, you will be one. If you want to be a great one, you've got to dream big. You are going to have to pay the price because that means you're going to have to work hard, you're going to have to work on your technique, you're going to have to be in great shape; otherwise you're going to fail. It has to become an obsession. Whether it is sports or work, at the end of the day you really don't work for the money, but the money is nice.*
>
> *Even in sports, achieving a title is great, but really it's about what you love and enjoy. Making it an obsession will help make you successful. You start with that, you dream big, and then you have to set goals. Goals help you track how well you're doing in terms of progress, and that tells you what you have to change in order to get to that next goal. One goal leads to another, so that you can achieve your dream.*

Leaders have to have a dream that is bigger than themselves, something they need the help of others to accomplish. Leaders push themselves and their organizations to greater and greater heights on the strength of their dreams. And even if they don't accomplish everything, as Michael Fitzpatrick points out, they still make it further than if they would have set their sights lower.

Dreaming big may sometimes feel audacious in the moment, but big dreams sometimes do become reality, as was the case for Jerry Oshinsky.

I ended up in law because, as a young person growing up in Jersey City, even though I did not have a lot of intellectual support or academic support, I was always a very good student. I remember thinking when I was really young that it would really be cool to build up my prestige by telling people, "I am going to be a lawyer." I had no idea what that meant at the time, but then when I was about twelve or thirteen years old, I read Clarence Darrow's autobiography. Clarence Darrow was one of the great American attorneys of the twentieth century whose famous trials included the Scopes Trial, among many others. Of course, he is the character portrayed as the defense lawyer in the play Inherit the Wind, which I was also in a few years ago.

I remember reading Clarence Darrow's autobiography and thinking, "I'd like to do that." I had no idea what it meant, really, to be an attorney, but from that point on, I decided that I was going to be a lawyer. I was always very good in liberal arts subjects, like English, history, political science, and literature. I always had the ability to read very fast and remember things that I read. So it just seemed like a natural fit for me . . . I knew what I was going to do from the time I was about twelve years old.

Jerry's big dream came from within, inspired by a role model who lived a hundred years earlier. Even though he had little intellectual and career support, that dream, coupled with his natural abilities, fueled a career that broke new ground in several ways, as we'll see in the next section.

Turn Your Dream into a Mission

Not only do leaders have to dream big, they have to focus that dream and shape it into a particular mission. An inspirational leader who is passionate about a dream and able to articulate it in the form of a focused mission is able to inspire others and organize the work of an organization toward a common goal.

Bissell has been a family-owned business for over 137 years. Here's how CEO Mark Bissell's passion and vision for a family business has translated into success:

We are a multigenerational family business, and over the years, the ownership of the company became spread out. I was able to pull back in a core group of family members who had a common agenda. I think that it is really important to keep the family company private. Most family businesses sell out because the agenda changes and family members get disassociated from the company. We have survived 137 years. Getting a few family members reconnected with the business and consolidating ownership was a big accomplishment. It will allow the business to continue for any number of generations, at least from a shareholder and succession standpoint. Other issues may come up, but that was a big one.

This has been a great business for many years, but now with an excellent management team, we were able to dramatically increase our market share to be number one in North America for floor care. We went from the middle of the road in terms of market share to number one in market share.

Mark was on the leadership team of Bissell because he was part of the family business. He could have chosen to do something else, or he could have chosen a more passive role within the company. Instead,

Mark chose to make the family business his life's mission. He saw it as a unique opportunity for his family, and a unique opportunity to create excellence within the business. He embraced the challenges of a multigenerational family company and made it his mission to put Bissell on firm footing for the next generation.

Some leaders like Mark discover their dream and their mission within an existing context. Other leaders, like Jerry Oshinsky, have to chart new territory. In many ways, Jerry followed the advice of legendary management expert Peter Drucker: "The best way to predict the future is to create it." In Jerry's own words:

> *I created the field of insurance coverage for policyholders. I sought insurance coverage from insurance companies for my clients in major well-known litigations involving all sorts of significant exposures, like asbestos, environmental, product liability, and director's office liability. In recent years the list has grown to include cyber exposure, hurricanes, and fires, and even sexual abuse and assaults.*
>
> *As a practice, it really is something that I more or less created, because before me, there was no recognized practice where somebody would represent policyholders against insurance companies. People did it, but it wasn't a core practice like securities litigation or government contract litigation. Now there are people who are known as insurance lawyers, not on the side representing insurance companies, but on the side representing the entities—the organizations, universities, cities, towns, or corporations—that are seeking insurance coverage for allegations of liability against them.*

Jerry saw corporate policyholders as an underserved sector of the market, and he shaped his vision into the practical mission of building a legal practice around this niche. In doing so he forged new territory and created the field of insurance law, which is now a specialty of its own with many practitioners.

Whether your mission is found, like Mark's, or forged, like Jerry's, sometimes the most difficult thing is to communicate that mission to others. An inspirational leader is someone who helps their staff connect the dots between their daily tasks and the bigger mission of the company. Communicating the big picture regularly will help reinforce the reason your organization exists and increase support from your team. (The next step to achieve your mission is to set meaningful goals.)

Be Self-Aware

We all have blind spots, but blind spots can be particularly costly to leaders. Mark Bissell explains,

> *I think being self-aware is really important. Everybody has weaknesses. Some are more obvious than others. In my position as the CEO and owner of the company, it is hard to get feedback. You have to go out of your way with a few trusted friends or advisors to say, "Hey, I need an honesty check—how and what am I doing?" Also, there are other things you can do if you really want a 360-degree review of yourself as a leader. Either way, I think it is important to be self-aware so that you know what your strengths and weaknesses are. And, like anything, try to deal with your weaknesses. It is not necessarily an easy thing to do. There is always something to be working on, but I think if you are aware of your weaknesses, you're more likely to be able to deal with them. I am always amazed that some people just aren't self-aware. At least if they are, they do a good job of hiding it. You are not doing yourself any favors that way.*

As we learned in the previous two chapters, everyone has strengths and weaknesses, and everyone makes mistakes. The same is true for leaders. The problem is that it's very hard to get honest feedback about your weaknesses and mistakes as a leader, because too often your employees or team members are going to tell you what you want to hear. So it's extremely important that you as a leader take responsibility for your own self-awareness. Do what you can to discover your weaknesses and mistakes yourself, ideally with the input of people you trust. Once you become aware of those weaknesses and mistakes, refer back to the previous two chapters: Surround yourself with the perfect team to compensate for those weaknesses, and always try to learn from your mistakes.

Face Your Fears

If great leadership comes from within, it should come as no surprise that some of the biggest obstacles leaders face are within themselves. How you handle fear will greatly impact your success as a leader. Here Greg Renker reflects on the fears he has faced and how he used his fears to propel his company forward:

> *Every day is a challenge, and some challenges are greater than others. You're always a little bit afraid. Even when you're doing well, you think your success is going to stop. The world is changing so fast that you are constantly trying to overcome new obstacles. You're also very aware of and a little bit afraid of competitors.*
>
> *Lawsuits in particular have been very scary. Early in the business, I was sued personally for a large amount. As the business matured, we got sued corporately. We've never lost any serious lawsuits, but they're not fun. We never sue. It usually takes someone else to start it.*
>
> *I would say the fear of the unknown is probably the biggest challenge we have faced—when you don't know the outcome.*

Projects you're working on . . . what happens if they don't work? If the projects are successful, what happens if they stop being successful?

I would say that fear is actually a really good motivator. It needs to be corralled and properly leveraged. We become what we think about.

Countless challenges can create fear in you as a leader: performance, projects, competitors, legal issues. The question is, what will that fear do inside of you? Are you going to dwell on it and allow it to cause you to freeze up? Or are you going use the fear as motivation to find a solution and move forward? Your leadership skills, your career, and your company depend upon what happens within you, so you need to lead yourself from within as well as your team.

True leadership comes from within, and it begins with dreaming big. Yet great leaders know that even the biggest dreams aren't enough; we have to focus those dreams into actionable missions, or visions that help us navigate our own career and coordinate the work of others. If we are not internally aware of our own weaknesses, we may be blind to the ways in which we are sabotaging our own dreams and mission. Finally, as leaders we have the responsibility to face our fears and use them to propel ourselves and our organizations forward.

Chapter 6
SET MEANINGFUL GOALS

I n the last chapter, we talked about the importance of dreaming big and turning that dream into a mission to accomplish. The next step is to set meaningful goals in order to make that mission a reality.

The goal-setting process is very straightforward, as long as you are honest with yourself. One of my high school coaches often told me as his athlete to "KISS SMART!"—that can mean more than one thing to a sixteen-year-old boy, if you get my drift.

By KISS, he really wanted us to remember to Keep It Simple, Stupid. To become successful as an athlete, his goal was to keep us from overthinking the situation and losing focus. He said if you can KISS, you will succeed.

By SMART, he wanted us to make our goals Specific, Measurable, Attainable, Rewarding, and Trackable.

KISS SMART was a memorable way for me as a young athlete to learn the foundation of good goal setting. As I interviewed my most successful clients to discover the foundation of their success, it was no surprise to me that they were all big goal setters and had some very specific things to say about the process.

Don't Reinvent the Wheel

To accomplish a mission, your goals need to be intentionally arranged to get you from point A to point B. Your specific arrangement of goals becomes something of a map. Whenever Greg Renker wants to do something new, he looks to see what maps already exist.

If our predecessors . . . have already done something that we want to do, they have already laid out a map. So the map is already there. In almost every single category, whether it's entertainment, music, business, or sports, the map is there to accomplish your goal.

As Greg said, the map is already there for you to accomplish your goal whether it is changing an industry, waking up earlier, or a creating a true rags-to-riches story.

In addition to learning from your competitors' mistakes and successes, which Greg discussed in chapter 4, he encourages us to read the great books of the last hundred years to find the proven roadmaps of success in any field (and he mentions the model for this book as well).

For example, Think and Grow Rich was written by Napoleon Hill, who was paid by Andrew Carnegie to go out and study how the five hundred most successful people in America at that time became so successful. He spent his career trying to figure out what science of mind enabled them to achieve all the great things that they did. He worked with everyone from Thomas Edison to Henry Ford. He concluded his findings in a book called Think and Grow Rich, which laid out the principles of success.

During this time, others were doing something similar. Dale Carnegie wrote How to Win Friends and Influence People, and later W. Clement Stone wrote The Success System that Never Fails. Can you imagine writing a book called The Success System that Never Fails? Who wouldn't want to read that book? So there are multiple top-quality books that have been written with the principles and fundamentals in them.

It's a little bit like Tiger Woods's book How I Play Golf. That's an outstanding book that starts from the very beginning in laying out the fundamentals and principles of how to play golf effectively. It's got it all in there; every tip, every technique, every foundational item is in there. Wouldn't you want to go through that book page by page if you were an aspiring golfer? So if you're an aspiring business person, or someone who wants to achieve their goals, wouldn't the same be true?

Within the pages of these books and others are maps that will help you set effective goals. From subjects as specific as golf to subjects as lofty as success, the maps are there and waiting for the price of a book and some of your time. Don't waste your time reinventing the wheel. Even if you don't follow another's path exactly, you will still set much more effective goals and go further and faster than you would otherwise.

Sometimes there really is no map, and you just have to discover it for yourself. In this case, you have to depend upon the principles that you can learn and the support of those who share that dream with you. Ema Boateng is a good example. He knew where he wanted to go from a very young age, but he just didn't know which road would take him there.

> *Starting at age twelve, my goal was just to play professional soccer right away—I thought I could play professional at that point. That was literally all I would think about.*
>
> *So at twelve years old I moved out of my house to play soccer for the Right to Dream Academy, one of the largest soccer academies in Ghana. They go around the entire country recruiting players, and out of three hundred candidates they choose sixteen. I stayed with those sixteen other kids for three years before I received a scholarship to go to high school at Cate at fifteen years old.*
>
> *I studied and played soccer at Cate for three years and decided to graduate a year early to play at the next level and start college early. Right now, I have a trip coming up to England and Sweden to try out with three different professional teams, including Manchester City. I've always been in contact with professional teams, going there to train with them. But that was all before I was eighteen, so I couldn't sign anything. Now it's a good chance to test myself and see if the next level is for me!*

No books and few role models could help Ema navigate from rural Ghana to professional soccer, but he still found his way.

Take Action Every Day

No matter how specific our goals may seem, they can almost always be broken down into smaller steps. Breaking down goals into smaller steps is also a great way to manage your stress and energy levels. You have twenty-four hours in a day but only so much energy. Make a plan, prioritize, and then tackle the most important items. Once you start chipping away at the project, it won't seem so unattainable. Don't let your e-mail inbox or little housekeeping tasks consume your day. That's not what will give you a raise. That's not how you get promoted. And that's not how you're going to be successful.

The three words that keep Patty Aubery going are "positivity, purpose, and passion." She makes these three words very practical by going on to say,

> Do the rule of five. Do five things a day to get you closer to the biggest goal you have. If you do that, and you do it first thing in the morning, you're on track.

I asked if she could give me an example from her own experience.

> One of our goals was to sell five million books by June or December of 1995. Every day when I would walk in my office, I would get out my rule of five card. I had these little cards that listed five things on there that I would write out the night before. It might be make a phone call to an editor, do a Newswire press release about the book, call someone and ask them if they'll promote it in their newsletter, or send out a link to a new page. Then, lastly, try to book an event where Jack could speak in front of one thousand people or more, or just make a call to one speaker's bureau. It could be anything. We just had to take action.
>
> I think a lot of people set goals, but they don't take action on those goals. You say, "Oh, I don't want to call that person right now," so you put it off, because it's uncomfortable to ask for things. I think the biggest thing that's made me successful is that I ask and I ask and I ask. I don't stop until I get a yes. No, for me, is so much fun. I love them. "Cool, I got a no. The next one is going to be a yes." I make it a game, so it's not about me and it's really fun. It's all about vision, and it's all about goal setting. Focus on what you

want, and not on what you don't want. I think people spend a lot of time worrying about things that they have no control over.

Patty's rule of five cards is a great practical way to break big goals down into small daily steps. Having the five goals for one day even allowed her to focus less on success or failure and turn something as unpleasant as rejection into a game.

As a trainer, I spend a lot of time helping people break down big fitness goals into daily actions. Here are six other tips I often give my clients to help them set effective, achievable goals:

1. **Write goals down.** This practice helps crystallize them and makes them real in your mind!

2. **Write each goal as a positive statement.** Putting your goals in positive terms helps energize and encourage you to meet them.

3. **Set realistic goals.** It's important to set goals that you can achieve. You may end up setting goals that are too difficult because you might not yet understand the obstacles before you, or how much skill you need to achieve a particular level of performance.

4. **Prioritize your goals.** When you're pursuing a lot of goals at once, setting priorities helps keep you from becoming overwhelmed. Each goal needs to be prioritized, and then you can focus on the most important ones.

5. **Be precise.** Precision is crucial for completing your goal. Set precise goals with dates, times, and amounts so that you can measure achievement and have the satisfaction of knowing when you've achieved your goal.

6. **Set performance goals.** Set goals based on what you can control, not the outcome! In business, you cannot control what others do, or the unexpected effects of economic trends or government

policy. In sports you cannot control bad weather, injury, or just plain bad luck. Basing your goals on personal performance will allow you to maintain better control over what you can control and be more likely to achieve your goals.

When setting goals, whether they are fitness, financial, or personal, these guidelines will help you stay on track. To start breaking down goals into actionable steps, pull out the "big picture" goals you listed back in the introduction of this book. Now you can break them down into smaller targets that you must hit in order to reach your lifetime goals.

Here is a hypothetical example about a marketing director to illustrate how this works. We will call her Cindy. One of Cindy's big career goals is to become senior vice president (VP) of marketing for the company she works for. Here's how she might break that down:

- Five-year goal: Become assistant VP.
- One-year goal: Volunteer for projects that the current assistant VP is heading up.
- Six-month goal: Get certified in a CRM marketing tool.
- One-month goal: Talk to the CEO to determine what skills are needed to do the job.
- One-week goal: Book the meeting with the CEO.

As you can see from this example, breaking big goals down into smaller, more manageable goals makes it far easier to see how the goal will get accomplished. Keep the process going by regularly reviewing and updating your goals. And remember to take time to enjoy the satisfaction of achieving your goals when you do so. If you didn't take the time to write out your big-picture goals earlier, go ahead and do it now. As you make this technique part of your life, you'll find your career accelerating, and you'll wonder how you lived without it!

Don't Give Up!

When you are trying to follow any kind of plan, whether you have charted a course for the moon or you are just trying to follow Patty Aubery's rule of five, it is easy to get discouraged and abandon your plan. Patty says,

> *Just keep on going. Don't give up. I think so many people have dreams and goals, and they want to be a success overnight. That never happens. It takes years to build brands and build people and companies. I just try to really encourage people not to give up.*

I remember having lunch with Angel Martinez and talking about running and overcoming the inevitable suffering that competitive runners have to endure. Bear in mind I was talking with someone who at one point could run a marathon in 2 hours and 18 minutes—that is running a little more than 26 miles at a pace just a little over 5 minutes per mile. I asked him, "How do you keep going in the middle of that kind of race?" He said,

> *All you have to do it just push it a little harder because you always have a couple extra gears that you may not think you have.*

Angel believes that you always have another gear, no matter how much you're suffering. You can always work a little harder. Angel applies the same mentality to the work environment as well.

> *It is all about the attitude. You've got to have that attitude that you can push it. You may not win every race, but if someone is going to beat you, then you can make sure that person has to work for it—whether it is a race, a job, or a competing company.*

You want to give it your all and dig into that extra gear. It's all about being tenacious. We instill that in our kids as well. My son's athletic and my daughter's starting to see that it's all about attitude too. It's just about the attitude of when you're challenged that you're going to dig deep and overcome it, which can definitely relate to the workforce as well.

Those who attain the rich life they want have the tenacity to not back down, to keep showing up, and to follow the plan regardless of how they feel on a particular day.

We have talked in previous chapters about the importance of dreaming big and having a mission, but setting and accomplishing goals is really where the game is won or lost on a daily basis. You can make the most of your goals if you follow tried-and-true maps laid down by other successful people who have gone on before you. Break your goals down into small, actionable items that you can complete on a daily basis. And, most importantly, don't give up.

Chapter 7
SWEAT EVERY DAY

A s I've said from the very beginning, the first six success habits we've covered so far are not new. You've probably seen them in some form in other books on productivity, leadership, and personal development. They are, to some extent, the fundamentals of success. However, all of the individuals profiled in this book have one habit in common that you don't often find in success literature today: They sweat every day.

Perhaps this fact should be no surprise, since many of them have come to me for personal training at one point or another. They are successful and fit. The question is this: Are they successful *because* they are fit? In this chapter you will hear these successful individuals answer that question with a resounding yes! They've convinced me that working out may be the little-known secret to success. Again, it's not that fitness alone will lead to success in all areas of life (hence the first six habits), but that fitness, when combined with the well-established fundamentals of success, is an important ingredient that holds everything together and even makes success worthwhile.

Fitness provides the foundation for sustained energy, clear thinking, stress management, and our ability to maintain our competitive edge. Remember, you only have one life and one body—treat them properly!

Fitness as the Foundation of Well-Being (and Wealth)

All the success in the world is meaningless if you die at age forty-one. That very thing nearly happened to Greg Renker.

> *At age forty-one, I had shortness of breath, so I went to three doctors and they said don't worry about it. I went to a fourth doctor, and he put me on a treadmill. He took me off the treadmill immediately. He called my wife and said, "I have to put a stent in your husband's artery." In the process of stenting three arteries, he perforated one, meaning he tore a hole in it. That caused me to go into code blue, which meant I flatlined. My blood pressure went to zero. Basically, I died on the table. The heart surgeon and cardiologist were in a circumstance they had never been in throughout their entire career. They had never popped an artery, and they never had to open up a heart cavity with an artery that was spewing blood. In effect, they performed a miracle in their own career.*
>
> *I woke up thirty-six hours later, heavily sedated with morphine, having had emergency bypass surgery at age forty-one. For the first month, I was pretty much told that if I was lucky, I might be able to walk aggressively again, but I certainly wouldn't be able to jog.*

Bear in mind that we had three boys. The doctor also told my wife that she should be prepared for the high likelihood that I would not make it to age fifty.

That singular event was the most rewarding health event of my life and always will be. That disaster—that fear-inducing, terrifying incident—triggered my commitment to health and fitness. It was where all my drive initially came from. Now my drive comes from the reinforcement and the joy of being fit. I am in a whole other place now—I can't imagine not working out.

For example, I'm trying to take one day off a week appropriately from exercising. It's the toughest day of the week. I'm tearing my hair out by four p.m., because my body and my mind so much appreciate being fit and moving. I get joy from just the sheer momentum of carrying forward. It's harder to be sedentary for me than it is to be mobile.

Greg came about as close as possible to not seeing the fruit of his labor in the advertising industry and not seeing his boys grow up. Whether you define success in terms of finances, purpose, or family, he almost missed it all.

Our physical well-being is the foundation of not only our ability to do anything in this life, but also our ability to enjoy doing it. Death is certainly the most dramatic example of losing our physical well-being, but every incremental loss of our well-being is an incremental death of our ability to live life to the fullest. We think a little less clearly. We have a little less energy. We are a little more susceptible to stress and depression. We have a little less capacity to create wealth, whether in terms of money or a rich life worth living. Our physical well-being represents our capacity to create wealth. In that way, physical health equals wealth.

Because of this, when Jim Corcoran mentors a new broker at Morgan Stanley, he teaches new brokers to tend to their physical well-being so they can be talented and productive over the long haul. He says,

> *I am an advisor at Morgan Stanley, but I make it a point to teach and mentor the younger brokers when they come in. I teach them how to become a fit human being and take care of themselves first. I think it leads to a better life and working harder, because you feel good about yourself, and it gives you self-esteem. It's a great way to get lost and forget about everything else, because if you don't get your workout in the morning, your day could be ruined.*

Morgan Stanley is a company that exists for the purpose of creating wealth in the narrowest sense of the word. By that I mean their clients measure the company's success in terms of dollars and cents. I find it fascinating that in such a competitive environment, Jim puts such a premium on his own physical well-being, and really sees teaching young brokers to take care of themselves as an investment in the company. Even if his clients only see the bottom line in terms of money, he knows that the only reliable route to consistent performance is to tend to his capacity to create wealth.

Fitness as an Antidote to the Modern Work Environment

Our modern work environment is a cesspool of stress and physical inactivity. These two poisons are a one-two punch to our health that leave us wide open to illness, insomnia, and depression. The meetings, the deadlines, the clients—they all cause stress, and without a physical outlet, that stress just builds up in our bodies. Exercise is the antidote to stress; it is a natural antidepressant, and it makes us sleep better at night.

Angel says,

Fitness or wellness or health, whatever you want to refer to it as, is a major stress-management tool. Just like today, after we are finished with this conversation, I'm going to go work out because it's been a tough day. Exercise has always been my relief valve for stress. It's better than any pill, I suppose, or any alcohol or anything like that. I have a very, very stressful job, so if I didn't have physical activity, I'm certain I'd find other ways to relieve stress. Most people end up eating and drinking, thinking that does it.

Eating too much and drinking too much alcohol just make the problem worse. They may make us feel better in the moment, but over time they will eat away at our health, which will only make us more sedentary and more susceptible to stress. It is an endless cycle that slowly strangles our capacity to create wealth.

There is a very strong correlation between your mental, emotional, and physical pain and stress. Your body holds on to all three of those stresses and creates pain and tension, which will create a lack of blood flow, sore joints and muscles, and muscle strains. Stress hormones like cortisol are heightened, which causes more inflammation in the body. This can lead to adrenal burnout. If you need to nap often, nod off at any free moment throughout the day, or fall asleep the minute your head hits the pillow, then you are probably on the verge of burnout and living in a pool of cortisol.

You may need a little rest and relaxation, and you may need to catch up on your sleep. However, you ultimately have to address the problem at its source. Sweat is the only antidote to the inactivity and the stress of the modern workplace. Sweat equals clarity. Sweat gives us the endorphins of a runner's high. If you want to be in the top 1 percent, however you define it, make sure you make a habit of sweating every day.

Fitness as the Competitive Edge

Many of the people I interviewed had been competitive athletes from a very young age, some playing in college and some playing professionally. It is not hard to see how a world-class professional marathon runner like Angel Martinez brings the same stamina into the business world. However, not everyone falls into that category. Mark Bissell got into competitive cycling well into his adult life. I asked him how he got into cycling, and he said,

> *I was probably about thirty. I was active when I was younger, but I was never a jock. I was not on the football team or the soccer team or anything like that. So a friend of mine from Colorado brought a new-fangled mountain bike—I just had a regular bike—and I went out riding with him on my Schwinn with the baby bike seat in the back. I was like, Wow, I really like this. We were just cruising around on the cross-country ski trails, and I really had a blast. I came home and got a specialized stump jumper, and I just fell in love with the sport. That was over twenty years ago.*

Mark didn't immediately get into professional cycling, and it was many years later before he put together a professional team. I asked him about competition, and if it helped him in business. He said,

> *I am driven by it. I do competitions in cycling, but I have friends who do a lot more. I like doing a couple of races because it is a good reason for me to maintain some kind of racing shape. But I try not to get too carried away with it because I try to stay in balance. It is fun, and I like to compete. It makes me push myself and I always want to do better, which translates into the business world. You have got to be competitive today. It is such a tough environment. There are huge opportunities with the marketplace that we are in,*

but that means there is more competition than there has ever been as well.

Competition is competition, and the challenges that Mark faces on the course help him face the challenges in the marketplace. In the previous chapter on goal setting, Angel said,

You want to give it your all and dig into that extra gear. It's all about being tenacious. It's just about your attitude when you're challenged, that you're going to dig deep and overcome it, which can definitely relate to the workforce as well.

Athletes look at challenges differently than nonathletes. They have a high tolerance for discomfort, a strong work ethic, and a certain reluctance to give up. Athletes bring this same competitive advantage into the workplace. Even if you don't compete, a firm commitment to a fitness program will instill the same virtues, helping you to develop a tolerance for discomfort and a powerful work ethic.

When fitness becomes a successful priority in your life, you become a leader to others as you provide an excellent role model. Being fit takes dedication and shows self-worth. You prove that you matter. You also demonstrate your discipline to stick with a program, no matter how difficult it may be. You have the stamina to overcome obstacles and make it across the finish line, a quality to be admired that can apply to every aspect of your life.

Although the first six habits are taught widely as foundational principles of success, I admit that I have never seen a success book list "working out" or even an investment in your physical health as a key component of success. But as you've seen, my most successful clients know that physical health equals wealth, and they count working out as one of their foundational habits for a rich life.

As a trainer who has a particular interest in corporate wellness and bringing workouts to the workplace, I know a lot of people struggle with prioritizing their physical health—even after they get over the wrong belief that they "don't have time" to work out. As we learned in the very first chapter, you have to make time for what's most important. In Part Two, you'll find my very best advice about how to incorporate this seventh success habit into your life for good—and reap the rewards!

Angel Martinez, now CEO of Deckers Outdoor Corporation, running.

Angel Martinez, now CEO of Deckers Outdoor Corporation, at the finish line of a race.

Angel Martinez, now CEO of Deckers Outdoor Corporation, on a partner run.

Angel Martinez, CEO of Deckers Outdoor Corporation.

Ema Boateng, now professional soccer player, as a baby in Ghana, West Africa.

Ema Boateng, professional soccer player, playing the sport he loves.

Ema Boateng playing soccer.

Ema Boateng, professional soccer player, receiving the Gatorade Player of the Year Award.

Ema Boateng with his family in the United States. Ema met Mark and Lynda Schwartz through their involvement with the Right to Dream Academy and have been family ever since.

Darya Pino Rose, author and expert of the science of healthy eating, sharing with us a delicious desert.

Darya Pino Rose, shopping at a local farmer's market.

*Greg Renker, co-founder of
Guthy-Renker, a world-class
direct marketing company.*

*Greg Renker enjoying
a game of golf.*

Greg Renker with his wife Stacey and their three sons.

*Will Chesebro, 2011 Team USA
para-cyclist, as a baby.*

*Will Chesebro, 2011 Team USA
para-cyclist, racing his bike
on the track.*

Jerold Oshinsky, renowned insurance lawyer, as a baby in 1946.

Jerold Oshinsky, known as the "father of insurance law."

Jerry Oshinsky with his family on vacation in Hawaii in 2015.

PART TWO

HOW TO MAKE
WORKING OUT PART OF
YOUR SUCCESS ROUTINE

Chapter 8
FOOD IS FUEL

The first step is to recognize that *food is fuel*. The better you eat, the better you will feel. It really is that simple. For the moment, forget about the Paleo Diet, or any other fad diet that you associate with healthy eating. Food is not a diet. Food is not a reward system. Food is fuel, plain and simple. If you don't give your body enough of what it needs, or if you give it a bunch of stuff it doesn't need, it is going to show up first in your energy level.

Food is fuel. Fuel is energy. And when you have energy, you feel good enough to tackle life's challenges, which leads to success in any context. People who understand this, like Greg Renker, Angel

Martinez, Michael Fitzpatrick, and Kevin Haley, are able to perform consistently at a very high level in every area of their lives. This is true whether they are on the job, in the gym, with family or friends, or just doing something they love. How you eat determines the "richness" of your life.

As a trainer, whenever I take on a new client the first thing I ask them is this: What do you eat? Sadly, many people can't answer that question honestly, because they honestly don't know what they are eating or how much. To get to know your own eating habits, I recommend keeping a food log for seven days every couple of months, especially anytime you feel like you need a reset. The bite of your kid's grilled cheese, the handful of almonds, the spoonful of peanut butter—they all add up fast! By keeping a log, you will force yourself to be conscious of what you are eating, and then you can make a commitment to make a change for the better.

To help you make those changes, we are going to talk first about the amount of food you eat, then about the kind of food you eat, and finally an overall meal plan.

Put Your Fork Down: Portion Control

You are the only one who picks the fork up, and you are the only one who can put it down. Base your portions on how active you are. If you are constantly traveling for work, or sit at a desk all day and only get sixty minutes or less of exercise a week, you don't need to eat that much. You might need 1,600–2,000 calories per day. Avoid simple carbohydrates like breads, and eat lightly. Now, if you are training for a marathon, then your needs are dramatically different. You also need to consume more carbs for energy so you don't bonk. Your level of activity determines how much food you need and how much of that food should be in the form of carbohydrates. Here are five simple tricks to help you with portion control:

1. When you go out to eat, take half of your food to go.
2. Buy smaller plates at home—your brain will perceive the portion to be larger if you fill up a small plate.
3. If you are starving before lunch or dinner, grab a healthy snack to hold you over: a few almonds or an apple.
4. Always order all salads with dressing on the side.
5. At restaurants, tell the waiter not to bring out complimentary chips or bread.

Clean (Your) Food

You can probably still hear your mother's voice in the back of your mind: Clean your plate! I would like you to replace that with another saying: Clean your food. Now I am not just talking about washing things like vegetables and fruit before you eat them, though that is certainly part of it. Clean food is food that is as free as possible from pesticides, preservatives, and all of the chemicals that go into processed foods. This is first and foremost a question of what kind of foods you purchase, and then a question of how you prepare them. If you can keep three words in mind when you are deciding what to eat, you will be well on your way to eating clean food: fresh, whole, and organic.

Here are some categories of clean food and what they can do for your body:

Any and all vegetables. This should be a no-brainer. Despite having this hammered into our heads since we were kids, the most eaten green food is pickles. Eating organic veggies is the healthiest option and the less you cook them the better. Avoid eating too many high-glycemic veggies like corn, carrots, and beets. Otherwise, eat vegetables frequently.

Greens. Dark leafy greens like chard, kale, spinach, and collard greens are all high in minerals, fiber, and vitamins. Remember, dark leafy greens provide the most concentrated source of nutrients compared to any food, which is why our ancestors ate four to six pounds of leaves a day!

Fruits:
- **Berries** give you a high source of antioxidants and fiber.
- Though extremely high in sugar, **bananas** help keep you full and energetic. They are also really high in fiber, vitamin B6, vitamin C, potassium, and manganese. For working out hard and sweating, potassium is a must—it helps maintain the fluid balance in your body.
- **Avocados** promote a healthy heart and are an excellent brain food. A typical avocado contains ten to fifteen grams of fiber and is high in healthy fats, vitamin K, lutein, and many other great things.
- Not only does an **apple** a day keep the doctor away, it delays fatigue in elite athletes, CEOs, and everyday people. Apples contain quercetin, as well as many other important nutrients such as creatine (for muscles), fructose (for quick energy), and fiber (for healthy digestion).

Eggs. Personally, I love egg whites, but I do recommend eating the whole egg when possible because the yolk is packed with healthy fats and nutrients. This decision would depend on your cholesterol levels, though, so you may want to discuss this with a healthcare provider. Regardless of whether you eat the yolk, try to buy cage free and organic— it does make a difference.

Fresh wild fish. If possible, just say no to farm-raised fish. Wild fish offers many more healthy nutrients. As a rule, the less time it takes for the fish to get from its natural habitat to your plate, the better.

Lean meat. By nature, we are meat eaters, whether it's chicken, red meat, pork, or turkey. Meats help build muscle and are important for our nervous system.

Yogurt. This does not mean processed, sugar-filled yogurt or frozen yogurt. It's best to eat plain Greek yogurts with live active cultures. Note: When checking the label, make sure bacteria was added after pasteurization, otherwise the bacteria is dead and useless.

Seeds and nuts. Some of the healthiest snacks you can munch on are almonds, cashews, walnuts, and pumpkin seeds. Remember to buy them raw and enjoy.

Grains. Good choices are wild rice, brown rice, and quinoa; they all are high in fiber and are digested slowly.

Create a Successful Mindset for Healthy Eating

I'd like to share with you a great conversation I had with Darya Pino Rose, PhD, an expert on the science of healthy eating. She's the author of *Foodist: Using Real Food and Real Science to Lose Weight Without Dieting* (HarperOne, 2013), and creator of the website Summer Tomato, which has been listed as one of *TIME*'s fifty best websites. She shared some very helpful insights not only about how to be successful at eating healthy, but about what it means to be successful in general.

Perry: What would you say are some of the biggest misconceptions about eating healthy?

Darya: Probably the biggest misconception in general is that eating healthy sucks. While everybody wants to be healthy, the word "healthy" has a very negative connotation for many people because of what they think you have to do to get healthy. When people hear the word "healthy," they think of not eating things they like, eating things they don't like, and working their butt off in a painful way at the gym. In fact, if your approach to getting healthy is primarily about sacrifice and deprivation, it is almost inevitable that you will fail.

Perry: Some say eating healthy is too expensive. Do you have any thoughts about that?

Darya: The idea that eating healthy is too expensive is one of the most common limiting beliefs about food, and it is really just an excuse to do nothing. Do you know what's really, really expensive? Being unhealthy for a long period of time. Think of the medical bills, insurance premiums, prescription medication, surgeries, and dying young. Not to mention all the discomforts of being sick for long periods of time and the difficulty of getting around. The cost of being unhealthy is astronomical, and short-term thinking can so easily dominate our mindset.

At the end of the day, sure—organic food is more expensive than conventional food. I don't think anybody would argue with that. However, vegetables are really the cornerstone of eating healthy, and vegetables are actually pretty cheap. What happens is that people will go to the farmer's market or they'll go to the grocery store, and they'll look at the organic food section. But they'll only really look at the fruit, and fruit actually is a lot more expensive than vegetables. You can get a cabbage for a dollar or less, and it lasts for days. It can be put into several meals. The vegetables themselves aren't that expensive, and at farmer's markets, organic produce is generally cheaper than grocery stores.

I think a lot of that is more of a mindset problem—that it's not worth investing in yourself, or that foods like cabbage are gross. But if you get a good cabbage from a farmer who cares, you learn how to cook it properly. It's not that hard. It's actually really delicious. It's one of my favorite vegetables. People who've made these changes quickly start to realize how delicious the food is, how easy it is, and how affordable it is. Then they don't even consider going back. But it's making that mental leap at the beginning that's really tough.

Perry: I have to ask, other than cabbage, what's your favorite vegetable?

Darya: Well, by far, my most popular recipe is for a roasted curried cauliflower. It has literally four ingredients: a head of cauliflower, some olive oil, some salt, and some curry powder, which is optional. The secret is to break the cauliflower and douse it in a good amount of oil and a good amount of salt. Then you cover it in foil and stick it in a really hot oven at 500 degrees. At that temperature, it steams for the first ten minutes. After ten minutes you take the foil off. You stir it, and then you stir it every eight to ten minutes for the next twenty to thirty minutes. It's really easy. I know kids who could do it. What happens is, at that temperature it gets crispy on the outside and still soft on the inside, and a little bit sweet because it condenses all the natural sugars in the cauliflower. And everybody says it tastes better than French fries. I always joke that it's my cauliflower that's better than French fries.

Perry: That sounds amazing.

Darya: It's so easy too. Even little kids will eat a whole head of cauliflower by themselves because they love it so much.

Perry: I'm going to have to try that later.

Darya: Me too!

Perry: What other objections do people have to eating healthy?

Darya: People tend to think that nutrition is really, really complicated. They think they need to be counting all these nutrients. Plus, the news contradicts itself from one week to the next. It's about this study and that study. What a lot of people do is just throw up their hands and say, "I can't do this. It's way too confusing, and I'd rather just eat mac and cheese."

What I try to do is just really, really, really simplify it for people. Because it doesn't need to be that complicated. When it's complicated, they're way less likely to do it. There are actually nutritional principles that we agree on, whether you're Paleo or vegan or something else. Everyone agrees processed food is bad for you. Refined sugars, refined fats, refined flour, processed meats—all those things are bad. Whether or not intact grains or natural meats are healthy, people will argue over left and right.

I tell people to focus on real food that looks like it comes from the earth—like a plant or an animal or a grain—and that's as minimally processed as possible. And you can apply the 80/20 rule to this. Try to get the majority of the food you eat from the category of real food. You can eat sugars and flours occasionally. You don't have to be dogmatic. You don't have to say, "I can never eat sugars." You don't have to say, "I can never eat meat." You don't have to say, "I can never eat chocolate or donuts." You can eat whatever you want. Just not every day. The meals that you eat every single day should just be made up of real food.

It comes down to creating habits. If you eat the same thing for breakfast every day, make it healthy. Make it something you enjoy. Establish healthy habits at the office. We spend a huge amount of time at work. If you can manage to establish healthy habits for the majority of the time, then on the special occasions, on the weekends, during happy hour, or whatever, you can live a little, you can indulge a little, and it's not that big of a deal. Focus on real food, especially for what you eat regularly. Save the treats for real special occasions.

People think they have to be perfect, and they feel really, really guilty if they aren't. It's just absolutely counterproductive. When they start feeling guilty and start feeling shame, a lot of people then go and comfort themselves with food. It just doesn't need to be that way. I'm living proof. I've got thousands of readers that are living proof.

The problem is most people eat 80 percent processed food. Sometimes processed food is branded as healthy—that national restaurant chain featuring submarine sandwiches is a great example. It's not healthy at all, but it gives the impression of being healthy. That's the trouble. We eat things like that and think we're making progress. However, if we'd just eat vegetables and eggs and meats and grains and beans and real foods, then we'd be fine.

Healthy eating is hard in the sense that a lot of us don't really have the skills to do it. If you didn't grow up in an environment where eating healthy was normal, then people are like, "What? I don't know how to cook. Where do I get these real foods? Is there a fast-food place I can go to get them?"

It's just as easy to cook healthy foods. It's not more expensive. It's not more work. The *change* is where the effort has to come in. The mindset change is hard work. Once you get there, it doesn't feel hard anymore. I think that's a huge barrier.

Perry: If it was easy, we would all be on our yachts looking like Brad Pitt and Angelina and not have to do anything! Nothing's easy. Some things are supposed to be hard work too.

Darya: Yeah—although in Europe, real food is a normal thing. That's why they don't have the health problems we do, at least in some places. The problem is that we totally outsource our food to a food industry that does not care one bit about our health.

We have allowed them to take over our food culture. Therefore, it seems hard to us because our normal is so skewed. We're really just trying to unlearn all that and get back to normal.

Perry: I think you hit the nail on the head. Let me change direction. Would you say that you are successful, and how do you define success?

Darya: I'm really happiest when I'm living in harmony with what I believe, and I feel like I'm making an impact on the things that I care about. I used to be in science. I got a PhD in neuroscience, and I was successful in that context. But I didn't feel like I was making a difference for other people.

I was studying a really small population of neurons in a mouse olfactory bulb, which is the part of the brain that makes them smell. Super, super minuscule stuff. It wasn't changing anybody.

Now that I have switched to writing, I get such real, tangible results. I literally get e-mails every single week from people telling me that I completely changed their lives. It might be somebody who read a blog post from several years ago and came back to tell me that they completely overhauled their workout habits or eating habits, and started their own blog or their own nutrition consulting thing. They were just writing to say thank you. That means success.

It has nothing to do with my number of Twitter followers or how much money I make. It's the feeling that it's making an impact. That's how I feel successful. That really gets it.

Once you're at the level of income where you're just comfortable and you don't have to worry about wilting all the time, more money is not that cool. It's not nearly as rewarding as actually feeling like you're making an impact.

Your Daily Meal Plan

In chapter 6, we talked about setting meaningful goals and the importance of making a map. Below are some ways you can take what you have learned about portion control and clean food and create your own ideal meal plan for the day, including breakfast, lunch, dinner, snacks, and drinks. Of course, there is a great variety of clean, healthy food available for you to enjoy, so please consider these options only as suggestions.

Breakfast

Have this meal as soon as you wake up to get your metabolism in gear. This meal should consist of good protein, healthy fats, and complex carbs. I know it is hard because we are always on the go, but try your best to include some vegetables in your breakfast.

- One cup of nonfat plain Greek yogurt topped with 2 cups of fresh strawberries and 2 hardboiled eggs (332 calories)
- One cup of instant oatmeal cooked with 1 tablespoon of natural peanut butter, then mixed with a scoop of whey protein powder (310 calories)
- One scrambled egg plus 2 egg whites cooked with 2 servings of spinach, then served with ¼ sliced avocado (250 calories)
- Smoothie made with 1 cup of frozen fresh berries, 1 cup of unsweetened almond milk, 1 serving of superfood powdered greens, and 1 scoop of whey protein powder (215 calories)
- One-half cantaloupe filled with 1 cup of low-fat 1 percent cottage cheese and topped with 16 raw almonds (285 calories)
- One banana topped with 1 tablespoon of natural peanut butter, served with 1 cup of water mixed with 1 scoop of whey protein powder (295 calories)

Midmorning Snack

You need a midmorning snack to sustain your energy throughout the morning and prevent you from eating too much at lunch.

- A handful of almonds or cashews and some fruit
- 2 to 4 ounces of chicken or turkey and a small piece of fruit
- Apple and a spoonful of peanut butter

Lunch

Do your best to avoid simple carbs after lunch—they will make you sluggish and tired. Remember to stay hydrated and drink more water if needed.

- Mixed green salad dressed with 2 tablespoons of low-fat balsamic vinaigrette and topped with a 6-ounce piece of poached salmon or chicken breast or 1 can of water-packed tuna, served with 2 corn tortillas (372 calories)
- Chicken sandwich made with 6 slices of chicken, ¼ avocado, 2 pieces of whole wheat bread, 4 slices of tomatoes, and some Dijon mustard for taste, served with a Gala apple (475 calories)
- Four ounces of grilled, cut, lean ground turkey served with ½ cup of brown rice, 2 servings of mixed vegetables, and topped with 1 tablespoon of Bragg Liquid Aminos (418 calories)
- Six-ounce burger made with lean ground turkey or a white chicken breast, wrapped in 4 pieces of lettuce with some Dijon mustard for taste, and a side green salad topped with 1 tablespoon of light balsamic vinaigrette (405 calories)
- Tuna salad with 1 can of water-packed tuna mixed with shredded red and green cabbage and sliced carrots, topped with sliced, roasted almond slices and dried cranberries, and dressed with 2 tablespoons of light balsamic vinaigrette (300 calories)

- One roll of sushi served with ½ cup of steamed edamame and a side salad dressed with light Asian-style dressing (445 calories)
- Fajita chicken salad made with mixed greens, 4 to 6 ounces of chicken breast, ¼ sliced avocado, ½ diced cucumber, ½ cup of corn kernels, 1 cup diced red and green peppers, and dressed with 2 tablespoons of light vinaigrette dressing (433 calories)

Afternoon Snack

An afternoon snack can pick you up so you don't have a midday crash at the office.

- Hummus and some raw veggies
- Perfect Foods protein bar (I like the low-cal flavors)

Dinner

Avoid starchy carbs at this meal.

- Six-ounce chicken breast grilled on stovetop or barbeque, served with 2 cups of broccoli and ½ cup of cooked quinoa (379 calories)
- Ahi salad with mixed greens on a ½-cup bed of brown rice, topped with 6 ounces of sliced sushi-grade Ahi, dressed with 1 tablespoon of olive oil and a fresh squeeze of lemon juice (522 calories)
- Shrimp stir-fry with 8 to 12 boiled shrimp mixed with 1 bowl of stir-fry vegetables, served with 2 corn tortillas (541 calories)
- Two rolls of sushi (tuna rolls) served with a small serving of miso soup and a cucumber salad (474 calories)
- Six-ounce grilled lean sirloin steak, ½ baked sweet potato, 12 grilled asparagus spears, and a side spinach salad with 1 tablespoon light vinaigrette (532 calories)

- Tofu stir-fry made with 6 ounces of tofu and broccoli, served on a ½-cup bed of cooked quinoa (505 calories)

Late-Night Snacking

I am not a huge believer in late-night snacking, because once you fall victim to this habit, it becomes really hard to stop. So, if you have a sweet tooth and need a little treat after dinner, try some of these options:

- Small piece of dark chocolate
- Handful of frozen grapes
- A cup of tea
- Unsweetened hemp or almond milk with some chia seeds

Drink Options

Remember, staying hydrated is a crucial part of staying energized, so be sure to drink enough water! Here are some healthy hydrating options:

- Minimum of 2 liters of water a day
- 1 to 2 cups of coffee a day (I prefer espresso to coffee)
- Herbal teas (just limit black and green because of the caffeine)
- Almond, hemp, and rice milk (try to avoid dairy)
- Avoid anything with artificial sweeteners, like diet soda (if you need a sweetener, try stevia; it's an all-natural herbal sweetener)

Learning to feed your body well is more than half the battle. If we jump straight to training schedules and proper lifting technique, I know from experience that we are just wasting time. Learning these principles of portion control, clean eating, and planning your meals will give you the energy, the stamina, and the confidence to approach your training schedule. You don't have to make this more complicated than it is, but you do have to do it. Remember, food is fuel. Fuel is energy. And energy not only feels great, but helps you create a great life.

Chapter 9
THE WORKBODY PROGRAM

As humans we have a broad range of physical abilities, including strength, power, speed, and endurance. Our ancestors were built to move frequently at a low intensity (nomadic activity), sprint when necessary (to catch food, or to avoid being food), and lift heavy objects. Ideally, these natural abilities allow us to do the things that we need to do in our physical environment with minimal risk of injury.

However, when we are stuck behind a desk for hours on end, travel constantly, relax in front of the TV, and generally find that our lives are characterized by long periods of sedentary activity, we slowly lose those natural abilities. Strength gives way to weakness, which leaves us prone to physical injury. One day you walk too quickly down the stairs and you are clutching your hamstring by the time you get to the bottom, or you reach for something on the top shelf and hurt your shoulder. You do things that you know the human body is more than equipped to handle, but from lack of use, your body has deteriorated to the point where even the simplest things can cause injury.

Unfortunately for most of us, the sedentary demands of our job are not going away. The desk, the computer, the car, and the airplane will continue to play a prominent role in our work lives. However, just because we cannot change certain aspects of our modern lifestyle does not mean that we have to give up on the areas that we can change. Humans have always depended on their natural ability to adapt to a changing environment.

I believe that we have to consciously adapt our behavior to accommodate the new demands of the workplace and preserve our natural strength, power, speed, and endurance. Doing so directly benefits us in the work environment in terms of increased energy, mental acuity, and ability to manage stress. We can't successfully adapt to this new work environment by simply taking the stairs instead of the elevator and parking farther away from the building (though I wouldn't discourage that).

We need a series of workouts that specifically addresses the shortfalls of our modern work environment, develops our core natural physical abilities, and is efficient enough to be done in a reasonable amount of time. This need led me to develop the Workbody Program.

Introduction to the Workbody Program

The Workbody Program is a combination of workouts that mimic some of the behaviors of our nomadic hunter-gatherer ancestors within the context of our modern society, helping us develop strength, power, speed, and endurance through *variety* and *functional fitness*.

Variety

An imaginative routine may not be a routine at all; environments, people, and conditions constantly change, and our workouts need to change with them. Variety is not only good for your training and body, but extremely beneficial for your brain too. No matter what obstacles, tasks, or work you need to do, there's always a way to incorporate some activity into them.

Functional Fitness

The Workbody Program focuses on functional fitness. Rather than isolating muscle groups or particular skills, we focus on exercises that combine muscle groups and work movement patterns that help you in your day-to-day activities, like running, climbing, or lifting heavy objects. Learning how to use your body the way nature intended it helps link all the muscles together, which prevents injury, allows you to maintain control, and reach new physical heights. Also, creating a sustainable exercise program that you can do anywhere with no equipment helps you maintain it even in your work environment.

The Program

The Workbody Program is made up of five different components:

1. Foundational exercises
2. Resistance training
3. Interval training
4. Long cardio
5. Rest and recovery

The key to the Workbody Program is to creatively combine these categories in a way that meets your own physical needs and fits within your work schedule. Some days your workout will draw on two or three different categories. Some days you may just focus on one category, like your long cardio. At the end of the chapter, I will show you how you can create an ideal week of training that balances all five aspects of the Workbody Program. But first, let's cover each category in detail, and along the way I'll show you some specific exercises and sample workouts.

Foundational Exercises: From the Ground Up

We've all heard the sayings, "You have to learn to walk before you can run," and "Rome wasn't built in a day." The Workbody Program is built on the same principle of progressive improvement.

As a trainer I have learned that most people cannot even control their own body weight, so why would I load them with weight right off the bat? Foundational training teaches people how to control, move, and activate their body properly, and this is key to sustaining a workout program and a low failure rate. Here are the "big five" foundational exercises I'd recommend for almost anyone.

The Big Five Foundational Exercises

1. **Lunge Stretch with Pulse.** In a deep lunge position with the right leg forward, shift all the weight to the back foot, squeezing the left glute forward. This will create a stretch in the left psoas and hip flexor. Once the stretch is initiated, interlock hands and reach arms overhead. Drop back knee slightly, keeping weight on back leg, and while pushing the left hip forward, pulse torso back 5 times. On the fifth pulse, hold torso back, then side-bend body toward right knee and hold 10 seconds. Come back to center and repeat 3 times. Switch legs and repeat.

2. **Wide-Feet Founder with Windmill.** Stand with your feet about 6 to 8 inches wider than your shoulders. Bend knees slightly, pushing butt back and heart forward, shifting all the

weight onto heels, to create a pull in hamstrings and glutes. Then, keeping shins vertical, squeeze heels and knees (your adductors) gently to create tension in the high-groin area and the inside of your legs. While keeping your heart forward, butt back, and shoulders away from your ears, engage your lats. Then reach arms behind you with palms facing forward and outward with spine extended. Hold for 15 seconds, then bring arms straight up above head with palms facing ceiling and hold 15 more seconds. Exhale and drop hands to floor, keeping knees slightly bent and weight on heels, trying to maintain a flat lower back. Lock left shoulder in, then unwind and windmill right hand towards ceiling for 10 seconds. Switch hands and windmill for 10 seconds. Then bring both hands back to center on the floor and create tension on adductors by squeezing heels and knees. Place hands on knees, press chest up back into starting position, and reach back for 10 seconds. Keep your butt tight and stand up.

3. **Goblet Squat.** Start with your hands at your side, feet shoulder-width apart, and toes slightly pointed out. Initiate movement by taking a big breath in through your nose and pushing hips back, bringing arms out in front of you as you descend. Once your hips cannot reach back any further, incorporate the knees by bending them to get closer to the floor. Keep body tight, chest up, and back straight, and pull yourself down into a squat. Never allowing knees to go over toes, hold in bottom position, making sure hips are pushed back, chest is up, and back is straight. Then place elbows between your knees and push out your knees with your elbows. Place hands together in a prayer position and hold this position for 10–20 seconds—this will create a stretch in the groin area. Next, reach arms overhead in a "Y" shape, push

hips back, and do 10 short pulses up and down. Then, place elbows between your knees again, pushing the knees out with elbows, and place hands together as in a prayer position and hold for 10 more seconds. During this hold, sway body from side to side 3–5 times to enhance groin stretch. Next, come back to center, take a big breath in, stay tight, and come up all the way, squeezing quads and glutes.

4. **Crossover Stretch.** Lie on your back with legs bent at the knee and your feet on the floor, cross the right leg over the left, and then pull legs to the right, trying to reach the floor. Create constant tension with knees to get a stretch in the left hip. Then straighten left arm at an angle behind you, keeping shoulder flush with the floor, and hold for 30 seconds. As you are holding, keep tension by trying to pull the left knee closer to the ground. Switch sides and repeat.

5. **Single Leg Founder.** In a deep lunge position with your right leg forward, shift all of your weight onto the right heel so that there is barely any pressure on the back leg. Keep front knee slightly bent in a split stance, with shin vertical and hips and chest up. Pull shoulders back and lean heart forward from hips until a stretch is felt in the right hamstring and glute. When you feel a good stretch, engage the lats, and while keeping shoulders away from ears, reach arms behind you with palms facing forward and rotated outward, spine extended. Hold for 15 seconds. Then bring arms straight up out in front of you and hold 10 more seconds. Then, with arms straight in front of you, turn to the right a few inches and hold for 10 seconds. Return to center, then turn to left a few inches and hold for 10 seconds. Come back to center, dig front heel into ground, squeeze glute, and stand up. Switch legs and repeat.

These five exercises are a great way to start teaching your body how to move properly, balance, and increase mobility and flexibility. It takes time and may feel extremely awkward at first, but moving pain free is worth the wait, work, and effort.

Functional Exercises

Other than the Big Five Foundational moves, one can also start with other functional fitness movements too:

- **Single Leg Split Squat.** Try standing on one leg on a stepstool perhaps eight inches high, and then lower the heel of your other foot to the ground while controlling your body weight as you go down and back up. Switch sides during each maneuver to promote balance and muscle integration on either side of your body.
- **Push-Up Negatives.** Go right into push-up position with hands directly under shoulders. Pull your shoulders away from your ears and engage lats, keeping hips up to engage core. Then squeeze glutes to tuck hips under body, staying completely tight. Take 7–10 seconds to come down, keeping core and body tight pulling body down with lats and leading with the chest, not the hips.

Try one and see if you can execute it with perfect form. Can you? They are harder than you think. Some people have isolated weaknesses that can cause a detriment in functional fitness and lead to injury, if not addressed first. If this is the case, why do so many of us skip the basics of learning proper control and go straight to moving too much weight too soon? It is not normal to be able to leg press 300 pounds, but not able to do a Single Leg Split Squat keeping the knee parallel with your shin.

Neither is it normal to be able to bench press 300 pounds, but not be able to do a push-up without your back caving in.

An everyday example would be a Bent-Over Row, but not the kind you do on a machine. I'm talking about hinging your hips back and letting your heart sit parallel to the floor, then with one arm holding the weight, pulling it up as your elbow points toward the ceiling. That exercise works everything—your core, back, glutes, and arms—plus you have to stay stable because you are performing it one arm at a time. Now compare that to a nurse bending over a bed to help a patient, or a car mechanic working on a car, or a contractor moving equipment. Can you see the similarity to many real-life situations? Contrast that to being in a machine performing a row with set levers and pads. Weight training goes beyond strengthening muscles. Your body needs to learn how to use itself by activating the core muscles and stabilizers in the back, arm, legs, and shoulders. If you don't use it, you will lose it!

Quick Tips
- Form is everything. Without proper form, you cannot have proper function, so remember: If you have a choice, always opt for working body weight and free weights instead of machines. You can have a much more neurologically demanding and intense workout.
- Never train to failure! You can still have intense workouts, but just don't go to failure; you are asking for an injury. Your set should end when you can no longer perform the exercise with perfect form.

If you work functional movements you innately are working isolated patterns as well. Therefore, instead of compensating and overusing certain muscles you can help your weaker muscles get stronger.

Once you can control and balance your own body weight, then you can start working with added weights. In lieu of adding weight, other popular tools to help create more functional movements are things like stability balls, wobble boards, dyno discs, bosus, etc. Start creating total body synchronization and teaching the upper body to work with the lower body.

Here are my top five functional exercises that you can do anywhere:

1. **Single Leg Split Squat.** See above.
2. **Side Lunges.** Stand with feet slightly wider than the Wide Feet Founder stance. Point your feet straight forward, keeping each arm pulled into your body like performing a row, creating a pinching effect in the shoulder blades. Initiate movement by pushing hips back and side lunge to the right side keeping left leg straight. Make sure weight is on the right heel loading the glute. The chest stays tall and is up. Hinge from the hips. As soon as you feel a stretch in the groin pull yourself back to center, and lunge to the other side. Do 5 reps per side.
3. **Spider-Man Push-Ups.** Start in push-up position with hands directly under shoulders. Pull shoulders away from ears and engage lats. Keep hips up to engage core, then squeeze glutes to tuck hips under body, staying completely tight. Keeping hips still, bring right knee toward your right arm, contracting the abs as you come down in a push-up—exhale and push yourself up. Repeat switching legs for a total of 10 reps.
4. **Back Extension.** Start on the floor, face down, with your feet together, elbows locked to the sides with palms facing down at shoulder level and hands off the ground. Keep glutes pressing into floor, draw shoulders down, and extend chest off floor 10–12 times. Keep feet on the ground at all times and chin tucked under you.

5. **Good Mornings.** Just as in the Founder, start by standing tall with feet about 6 inches apart keeping weight on heels. Bend knees slightly keeping shins vertical. Place two fists in between knees and squeeze until you feel the pull in the adductors and high-groin area. Keep that tension and place hands onto knees and press your chest up to engage the lats, keeping shoulders away from ears. Pushing hips back, cross both arms in front of your chest. Staying tall, keeping legs bent about 30 degrees, move from the hips and push the butt straight back (folding from the hips, not the back) allowing the heart to fall forward so the spine stays extended. As soon as you feel a stretch in the hamstrings and glutes, come up by pushing through heels and squeeze quads and glutes at top of motion. Keeping body tight, repeat for 12–15 reps.

Get Your Rear in Gear

The rear, also known as the ass, butt, booty, and posterior chain, is a very powerful and underutilized tool that can be used for something other than sitting. Your glutes in particular are not only your driving force for power and movement, but they also provide a major part of your core strength—and are likely underused if you find yourself sitting a lot. Listed below are five targeted exercises to get your rear in gear, which include some rehab and foundation exercises, strength exercises, and kettle exercises.

1. **Hip-Up Glute Bridge**. A glute bridge is performed while lying on your back with arms placed at your sides, keeping your palms down toward the ground. Place your feet about 10 to 12 inches away from your butt, allowing your knees to bend to a 45-degree angle. Keep your feet and knees about 6 inches apart, about as wide as both of your fists. Then clench your glutes as

if you're using them to pick up a quarter, and elevate your hips towards the ceiling. Hold this upright position between 2 and 3 seconds, come down, and repeat for 10 repetitions.

2. **Good Morning Stretch.** Say good morning to a strong lower back and hamstrings, and bye-bye to nagging back pain and stiffness. This exercise can be performed without any equipment. Start by placing your feet shoulder width apart with a slight bend in the knees. Keep all of your body weight in the heels of your feet, and keep the chest and torso nice and tall. Then place your hands behind your head, and hinge your hips back, allowing the torso to move forward. Keep the abdominals compressed and draw your navel in. Bend down until you feel a slight stretch in the hamstrings and glutes, and then hold for 30 seconds. Then re-engage your glutes by contracting them and pull yourself back into an upright positon.

3. **Kettlebell Swings.** The kettlebell swing is the foundation exercise for all kettlebell exercises, and to perform this exercise properly, you must squeeze your glutes and keep constant tension in your abdominals. As with any exercise, you must progress to this one; sumo-wall squats and deadlifts are a good way to do that.

4. **Hip-Up Glute Bridge Hamstring Curls.** Similar to the Hip-Up Glute Bridge described earlier, this exercise requires core stability and strength. Again, start by lying on your back, placing your arms at your side with palms facing down. Then, extending your legs straight out, place the heels of your feet on a stability ball. In this position, squeeze your glutes and raise your hips off the ground. Once the hips lift up, roll the ball toward your glutes while trying to keep your hips off of the ground. Repeat this motion of rolling the ball back and forth for 10 repetitions.

5. **Step-Ups.** We have all walked up and down stairs or bleachers at some point in our lives. The step-up is just a controlled variation of this. To perform this movement, place one foot on a bench, step, or box, and step up, keeping your abs contracted and shoulders back. The key to this movement is to fully extend the leg that is on the bench before you begin coming back down toward the floor. Perform 10 repetitions before switching legs.

Resistance Training

The resistance training section of the Workbody system is built on the principles of *circuit training*. Circuit training breaks up the monotony of old-school weight lifting and makes workouts more efficient and fun. Resistance and strength training two to three times per week will help build muscles, prevent muscle loss, and slow the aging process. So, how do you create the most efficient, energy-packed, strength-building circuit?

Work the Movements, Not the Muscles

Circuit training focuses on working movement patterns rather than specific muscle groups to create true functional fitness and long-term success. This approach will keep you injury free and create a balanced weight routine. When you combine these six movement patterns, you have a complete workout:

1. **Vertical Push**. This movement pattern includes movement in the upward plane of motion, exemplified through any overhead pressing motion. Shoulder press and lateral raises are two examples that target this pattern.
2. **Vertical Pull**. This action focuses on all overhead pulling motions. Exercises that fall into this category include chin-ups, pull-ups, and pull-downs.

3. **Horizontal Push**. This pattern includes movements that push in the horizontal plane. Examples are push-ups, bench presses, and all of their variations.

4. **Horizontal Pull**. This pattern includes all pulling motions in the horizontal plane. This includes rowing and all of its variations.

5. **Hip Dominant**. This pattern is often neglected. It targets the glutes, hips, and hamstrings, which is also referred to as the posterior chain. Exercises include step-ups, bridging, deadlifts, and kettlebell swings.

6. **Quad Dominant**. This pattern, which includes squats, lunges, leg presses, and their variations, focuses on the thigh muscles (quadriceps).

By equally hitting all six of these movements in a single workout, you will be able to create a balanced, full-body strength routine in minutes while including a full compound of movements and multijoint exercises. Our goal is to create the most metabolic demand during the workout and, most importantly, stay injury free.

Basic Principles of Resistance Training

Before we get to the actual workouts, I want to share a few other basic principles of resistance training:

- Keep in mind that resistance and strength training is a skill, so always focus on form and technique. When lifting heavy, keep perfect form and never lift to failure (i.e., lifting until you can't complete a repetition). Stopping a couple repetitions (reps) before muscle failure and losing form will allow you to recover and progress faster.

- Keep count and keep track of what you are doing.
- Hit all energy systems—strength, power, and endurance—by varying the number of sets and reps. A general rule of thumb is the fewer the reps, the higher the sets—and vice versa. For instance, I recommend that my clients aim for 12 to 20 reps per exercise. One day you may do 10 rounds of 2 reps each, while another day you may do 4 sets of 5 reps a piece. Rep range depends on what your goal and intensity/load level is for the set (whether strength, power, or endurance). Strength range is 1 to 5 reps, power range is 1 to 5 reps with less weight than strength, and endurance range can go as high as 20 to 30 reps. By the way, it is okay to do less reps and more weight. There is an urban myth that lifting heavier weights will bulk you up—women, I am talking to you! This is not true at all. Lower rep numbers actually build muscle *strength*, not mass. Remember, you can only have two things: muscle or fat. You choose!
- Form is everything. You must learn body awareness so you can control your tension. Keeping and controlling tension will help decrease power leaks, stabilize your body, and increase strength gains, even with the lightest weight or no weight. Plus, it keeps you injury free.

How to Design a Resistance-Training Gym Workout

When I design a resistance-training gym workout for a client, I always follow the same basic pattern:

- Warm-up
- Core
- Strength circuits (two or more)
- Cardio intervals

Each strength circuit focuses on two or more of the six movement patterns above: vertical push, vertical pull, horizontal push, horizontal pull, hip dominant, and quad dominant.

Three Sample Resistance Workouts: Beginner, Moderate, and Advanced

Here are three sample resistance workouts that all follow the pattern above: warm-up, core, strength circuits, and cardio intervals. There is a beginner workout, a moderate workout, and an advanced workout.

Because I wanted to keep this book as clear and as easy to understand as possible, rather than write out instructions for all of the exercises listed below, I've done full video demonstrations for each of the workouts that follow. You can find these videos at www.workoutandgrowrich.com.

Beginner Workout

Basic Warm-Up (2 times through)
- Side Lunges: 5 reps per side
- Mountain Climber Stretch: 3 to 5 per leg
- Hip Walks: 15 steps to left, 15 steps to right.
- Squat into Goblet Squat: 5 reps, hold for 10–20 seconds, 10 pulses
- Wide Feet Good Mornings: 15 reps

Core (1 time through)
- Roll-Ups: 10 reps
- Teaser Crunch: 15 reps, switch leg position, then repeat
- Side Twists: 7 twists to each side
- Side Planks: 30 seconds each side
- V-Ups: 5 to 8 reps
- Walkout Hold: hold for 15 –20 seconds

Strength Circuit One (3 times through)
- Pull-Up or Pull-Up Negatives: 5 reps
- Controlled Step-Downs: 5 per leg
- Push-Up or Push-Up Negatives: 5 reps
- Hip-Up Bridges: 15 reps

Strength Circuit Two (3 times through)
- Weighted Mini-Squat Press: 5 reps
- Side Lunges: 5 per side
- Mission Impossible Row (TRX straps): 10 reps
- Squat Double Body Weight (at first): 10 reps

Cardio intervals (2 times through)

On elliptical, treadmill, or rower:
- 30 seconds easy, 30 seconds at 80 percent effort (2 times)
- 1 minute easy, 1 minute hard at 80 percent effort (1 time)

Moderate Workout

Warm-Up
- Use the above Basic Warm-Up or a variation of your own

Core (2 times through, or 8 minutes)
- Hanging Leg Raise in straps: 5 per side and 5 straight up
- Side Planks: 10 dips and 10 scoops per side
- Full Sit-Up, reaching up, with 20–45 lb. weight (something holding your feet down): 10 reps
- Front Plank Rollouts on Balance Ball: 10 reps

Strength Circuit One (12 minutes)
- Pull-Ups: 2 reps
- Shoulder Press: 6 per arm

- Two-Arm Bent-Over Row: 12 reps
- Decline Push-Ups: 6 reps

Strength Circuit Two (12 minutes)
- Deadlifts: 2 reps
- Front Squats with Barbell, Kettlebells, or Dumbbells: 6 reps
- Kettle Swings: 12 reps
- Weighted Side Lunges: 6 per side

Cardio intervals (2 times through)
- Pick your machine:
- 1x 1 minute hard, 1 minute easy (2 times)
- 30 seconds hard, 30 second easy (1 time)

Advanced Workout
Warm-Up
- Use the above Basic Warm-Up or a variation of your own

Core (4 times through or 6 minutes)
- Ab Wheel: 5 reps
- Hanging Leg Raises in Straps: 15 reps

Strength Circuit One (4 times through, or 6 minutes)
- Weighted Pull-Ups: 2 reps
- Band-Assisted Piston (butt to floor): 2 per leg

Strength Circuit Two (4 times through, or 6 minutes)
- Lunge and Single-Arm Press: 2 per arm
- Barbell Deadlift: 2 reps

Strength Circuit Three (4 times through, or 25–30 minutes)

- Single-Arm Kettlebell Ladder (5/3/1):
  - o   5 press, 5 snatch, 5 squats
  - o   3 press, 3 snatch, 3 squats
  - o   1 press, 1 snatch, 1 squat
  - o   Switch arms
- Kettle Swings: 15 reps
- Assisted Pull-Ups: 15 reps
- Alternating Hands Med Ball Push-Ups: 20 reps total

Cardio intervals (1 time through)

- 500 meter row at 80 percent
- 0.25 mile on elliptical at 80 percent
- 500 meter row at 80 percent
- 0.25 mile hill level 4 run at 80 percent

Interval Training: Burn Fat Fast

Interval training is hands down the most efficient, stimulating, and effective way to perform cardio. The short bursts of high intensity keep you from dreading every remaining minute of your workout.

Intervals are just bursts of intense activity alternating with periods of easy recovery. Like everything, variety is the spice of life, so it's good to switch between shorter, more powerful intervals of 15 to 60 seconds and longer less intense intervals of 2 to 12 minutes. In the sample workouts below, I refer to the intensity of the interval in terms of a percentage, so an interval performed at 95 percent intensity would be performed at nearly maximum exertion. I recommend that a typical interval workout should be anywhere from 15 to 30 minutes long, depending on the day, workout, and intensity. I prefer to do my hardest intervals at the end of a strength workout, because I feel like it makes you a fuel-burning machine all day long!

Regardless of the type of cardio workout, it is critical to warm up properly. For each of the workouts, always begin with 3–7 minutes of easy, low-impact, and low-resistance movement. Try to maintain a higher or faster turnover (i.e., stroke, stride, cadence, or pull per minute, depending on your activity). Remember, all we are trying to accomplish here is to get the blood flowing before the workout. I recommend that following that 3 –7 minute warm-up period, perform 3 to 5 sets of 30-second controlled sprints, using moderate resistance, with 60 to 90 seconds of rest between intervals. This is a great way to conclude the warm-up, get out all the "yeah, yeahs," start sweating, and raise the heart rate. After this warm-up, you will be ready for any workout.

Note: Because all of the sample interval workouts listed below use percentage effort to gauge intensity, they are appropriate for any fitness level.

Three Interval Workouts for the Elliptical Machine

Workout 1: Pace Change Intervals (27 minutes total)
- Do 2 minutes at 75–80 percent effort (set resistance at a medium difficulty and try to keep strides high)
- Recover for 1 minute
- Do 4 x 30 seconds at 90–95 percent effort with 30 seconds of rest in between (set resistance a bit higher than 2-minute interval)
- Recover 2 minutes
- Repeat entire set for a total of 3 rounds

Workout 2: Mixed Pace Intervals (18:30 total)
- 3 x 1-minute interval at 80 percent effort with a 1-minute recovery (set resistance at medium difficulty while maintaining a high stride)

- 3 x 30-second intervals at 85 percent effort with 1-minute recovery (resistance is set a little higher because sprint is a little shorter)
- 3 x 15 second intervals at 90 percent with a 45-second recovery (push these a little harder and increase the resistance a bit more)
- 2 minutes easy
- 3 minute time trial (all-out effort for time)

Workout 3: Descending Intervals (18 minutes total)
- 2 x 2 minutes at 80 percent effort with 1-minute recovery
- 2 x 90 seconds at 80 percent effort with 1-minute recovery
- 2 x 60 seconds at 80 percent effort with 1-minute recovery
- 2 x 30 seconds at 80 percent effort with 1-minute recovery

Three Interval Workouts for the Treadmill

Workout 1: Time Trial
- Run or walk at 80 to 90 percent intensity for 15 minutes. Track your average speed and total distance. See how much farther and faster you get as you get fitter.

Workout 2: Hill Repeats
- Do 6 x 45 seconds at incline 5 to 7 percent at 75–80 percent with a 1-minute recovery.
- Do 6 x 30 seconds at incline 5 to 7 percent at 85–90 percent with a 1-minute recovery.

Workout 3: Flat to Steep Intervals
- Do a 1-minute flat interval at 75–85 percent effort.
- Go right into a 1-minute hill interval at 6 to 8 percent incline at 75–85 percent effort.
- Recover for 1-minute, then repeat for 5-8 intervals.

Three Interval Workouts for Rower or Concept 2 Ski Erg

Workout 1: 500 Meter Repeats
- Do 4-8 x 500 meters at 75–80 percent effort with a 1-minute recovery.

Workout 2: Power Set
- 2 x 250 meters at 85–90 percent with 1-minute recovery
- 4 x 100 meters at 90–95 percent with 30-second recovery
- 2-minute break
- 2 x 250 meters at 85–90 percent with 1-minute recovery
- 4 x 100 meters at 90–95 percent with 30-second recovery

Workout 3: Threshold Set
- Do 8–10 x 250 meters at 80–90 percent effort with 30 seconds of recovery between sets. Try to maintain a hard and sustainable pace for all of them.

Intervals are a great way to introduce variety into your workouts, have fun, and burn fat as quickly and efficiently as possible.

Long Cardio

We were made to move. The point of longer cardio is to keep you moving and therefore everything in your body flowing properly. Be sure to change up your longer cardio activities. You want your exercise not only to count but to pay dividends, so you certainly don't want to feel like you're in a rut. Here are some ideas to increase your heart rate, pump up your metabolism, and have fun while working out.

walking	swimming	jump rope
boxing	aerobic dance	kickboxing
tennis	row or ski erg	versa climber
soccer	spinning	circuit class
stepmill	surfing	paddle boarding
cycling	elliptical machine	squash
water aerobics	yoga	foundation exercises
skiing	in-line skating	cross-country skiing

Get outside, learn a new activity, or play a competitive sport—this is your opportunity to enjoy being fit. I recommend at least one hour of long cardio a week.

Rest and Recovery

In the Workbody program, rest and recovery is a lot more than doing nothing. Elite athletes are intentional about what they do for rest and recovery, and you need to learn to recover like the best.

Here are my top six rest and recovery tips, which will help ease muscle pain, relax your muscles, and speed up recovery:

1. Have a professional do tissue work
2. Get lots of sleep
3. Walk or spin on a bike at a relaxed pace to loosen up
4. Use a foam roller for self-massage
5. Ice sore areas
6. Take a cold plunge in an ice bath or ocean

Similar to professional athletes, I believe everyday people should have a team of massage therapists, chiropractors, and physical therapists ready to help them relieve the muscle pains and aches caused by the work environment. I know this is not feasible yet, but hopefully one day these dynamics will change..

In the meantime, a simple remedy to help relieve muscle tension is to incorporate a foam roller and a softball into your daily routine. A foam roller is just a dense cylinder ranging from 5 to 26 inches in length that you can use to apply pressure and create your own soft tissue massage. Many of my clients call it "the poor man's massage." Foam rollers range from $18 to $35, depending on what length, brand, and quality you prefer. I always recommend the Trigger Point foam roller, because its 5-inch roller is great for travel and the office. The idea is to increase blood flow to knots and tender spots in order to help the muscles move more fluidly. It might feel strange at first, but I encourage everyone I work with to foam roll for 10 to 20 minutes a day as a warm-up, workout, lunch break, or cool down from your workout.

A cheaper, more precise tool is a softball, which works great for all the trigger points and can easily be used while working and traveling. I am reminded of a CEO client of mine who is extremely fit and active; he is always running, lifting, or stand-up paddling. He complained of having tight glutes and struggled to maintain good posture because he was always in a car, behind a desk, or on a plane. One morning after a workout I gave him a softball to use for his long drives and flights. He gave me a look that said, "What the hell is this for, Perry?" I told him how he could benefit from using the softball on his glutes, shoulders, and even neck as he travels. To this day, eight years later, he still has the same softball in his car.

The Foam Roller Workout

This workout has become a staple in my routine. I try to do it every night before bed, especially when traveling, to rid myself of knots and ensure a higher decompress after work. Just turn on the television, tune out, and roll out your happy spots (because you're happy once you are off them)!

1. **Glute/hamstring**. Start by sitting on the foam roller, with hands placed behind you and your legs bent. Place all weight on one glute. Use the opposite foot to move back and forth on your tender spot for 30 reps; then fully extend the same leg and roll the roller on the hamstring. Roll from the bottom of your butt to the top of your knee, rotating your leg at different angles to get all sides of your hamstring. To enhance the stretch, place resting leg on top to create more weight on tender spots. Complete about 30 reps up and down, then switch to other glute and hamstring and repeat.

2. **IT band (muscle on outside of your quad).** Place roller on the outside of your upper leg right above the knee; use your elbow or hands for support. Roll from the top of knee to your hip and hold each tender spot for 10 seconds, trying to use your breath to release the spots. Complete 15 reps up and down leg, then switch sides and repeat.

3. **Quads.** Lie on your stomach in front plank position, with roller right above your knees. Roll from top of knees up toward your groin. To enhance, do one leg at a time. Hold each tender spot for 10 seconds. Try to use your breath to release the spots. Complete 15 reps up and down leg, then switch sides and repeat.

4. **Calves**. While seated on the floor, extend both legs straight in front of you and place roller under your left calf. Cross your right leg over your left. Using your hands as leverage and support, lean back and roll up and down the calf about 20 times. Then rotate your leg to the inside and roll about 20 times. Finally, rotate your leg to the outside and roll about 20 times. Switch legs and repeat.

5. **Lats**. Lie on your left side and extend your bottom arm straight out, then place roller horizontally below your chest right under your armpit. Keep your heart up and roll past your armpit and shoulder and back down 20 times. Switch sides and repeat.

6. **Pecs**. Lie on your stomach and place roller under an extended left arm with the end of the roller under your armpit at the top of your chest. Roll back and forth 20 times. Switch sides and repeat.

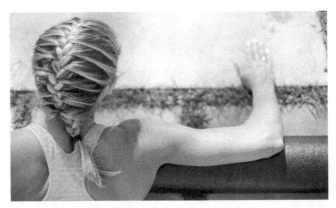

7. **Lower back**. Lie down faceup, with knees bent and feet planted firmly on the floor to support your weight. Place the foam roller under your lower back. If you are able, fold your arms across your chest. If not, use your arms to gently support your weight on the ground. Slowly roll over your lower back. If you find a sore or tight spot, hold roller for 30 seconds, then continue to roll gently back and forth to alleviate remaining tension. Repeat until all sore or tight spots are addressed.

8. **Upper spine**. Lie down faceup, with knees bent and feet planted firmly on the floor to support your weight. Place the foam roller under your upper back. Pressing your feet into the floor, slowly roll the foam roller up and down over your upper to middle back. To increase the pressure, press more of your weight into the roller. When you find a tight spot, hold for 30 seconds, then slowly roll and increase pressure to alleviate remaining tension. Lie down faceup, with knees bent and feet planted firmly on the floor to support your weight.

Before we leave the topic of rest and recovery, just one final word about sleep. Depriving yourself of sleep is a serious matter. There is a direct correlation between obesity and sleep disorders: If you don't sleep enough, you won't produce enough of the appetite-suppressant hormone, which will cause you to be hungrier all day. Remember that the amount of time you sleep is just as important as the amount of time you spend awake, so don't sell yourself short.

The Perfect Week

Now it is time to take these five components (foundational, resistance, interval, long cardio, and recovery) and combine them into the perfect week for you.

If you don't already have a daily workout routine, the first thing you'll need to do is decide when you're going to work out. As I mentioned in chapter 1, I believe the best time to work out is in the morning—even if you consider yourself a night owl. Early morning workouts offer special advantages. Your body produces more adrenaline at the start of the day, and that adrenaline helps power you through intense cardiovascular routines. Additionally, scientific studies have demonstrated that morning workouts lead to fewer food cravings, which in turn leads to weight loss. And morning workouts also give you more energy throughout the day—all the better for tackling business challenges.

In terms of the specifics, I believe that a person should do resistance training 3 days a week, cardio of some sort at least 3 or 4 days a week with different intensities and lengths, and recovery or foundation workouts 1 or 2 days a week. Remember, it is okay to go outside and get some fresh air for your intervals and longer cardio; being outside makes your workout more enjoyable, and the more you enjoy it, the longer you'll likely go—making it easier to build endurance. It's much better to do an activity you enjoy rather than feel like you have to sit on a bike for two hours reading a magazine.

Finally, there is no such thing as makeup days. Don't be a slave to your schedule and your routine, no matter how ideal it is. If you miss a day, let it go and start again tomorrow. Also, listen to your body. If you don't feel good after about 10 or 15 minutes, stop the exercise and walk away. It is not just a matter of managing your time; you have to learn to manage your energy and your fatigue as well. If you are not feeling good after your workout, you are probably not progressing anyway. Evaluate what you are doing as you are doing it; your goal is not to punish your body during every workout.

So here is a suggestion of what a perfect week could look like:

Sunday: long cardio (1 hour)
Monday: foundational (20–40 minutes) or day off
Tuesday: resistance training (30 minutes) | intervals (15–20 minutes)
Wednesday: recovery day
Thursday: resistance training (30 minutes) | intervals (15–20 minutes)
Friday: foundational (20–40 minutes)
Saturday: resistance training (30 minutes) | intervals (15–20 minutes)

However you decide to do it, if you want a life rich in health, wealth, purpose, and happiness, you have to find a way to make exercise an integral part of your life. Develop a schedule that works with the demands of your life and energy levels throughout the day and week. Staying healthy and fit is a choice you have to commit to—if my clients can fit it into their schedules, you can too!

Chapter 10
PUTTING IT ALL TOGETHER: TWO CASE STUDIES

n Part One, we covered seven habits that successful people integrate into their lives, including the one that almost never makes the list—fitness. In Part Two, we took a deeper dive into fitness, breaking it down into two components: nutrition and exercise. It is a lot to take in, and it is easy to get overwhelmed and lose sight of the whole. So here at the end of the book, I thought I would include two case studies of people that I think do a phenomenal job of integrating all of this into their daily lives.

They are both incredibly successful, but each in their own unique way. In some respects, they are at opposite ends of the spectrum.

One is a successful entrepreneur and businessman. The other is a professional watersports athlete who spends most of his days in the waves of Maui. Everyone has their own idea of what success means to them, and my guess is that your definition of success falls somewhere between these two individuals. Regardless, I think you will find both stories inspiring. They were both gracious enough to allow me to interview them, and I have included both interviews below as case studies in success.

Ed Snider

Ed Snider is one of the most influential people in the world of professional sports in Philadelphia, and one of the most inspirational people I know. He bought the franchise that began the NHL team the Philadelphia Flyers, and for a time he owned the NBA team the Philadelphia 76ers. He is the chairman of Comcast Spectacor, which now owns the Philadelphia Flyers, the Wells Fargo Center in Philadelphia, Comcast SportsNet, and Global Spectrum.

I know Ed as a very fit and dedicated friend and client. I met Ed when I was nineteen years old covering for a fellow trainer on leave. I thought Ed was in phenomenal shape for someone in his fifties (I found out later he was actually in his seventies). In those first few sessions training Ed, I found myself just asking questions and wanting to learn more and more about him and his story. I was amazed by his work ethic and his ability to take risks and capitalize on opportunities, which you will see in the interview below.

Perry: Let me start by asking how you got to where you are today.

Ed: I wish I knew.

Perry: I have such vivid memories of the stories you would tell me when I was your trainer. Stories about how you got started by selling records at grocery stores, and how things unfolded from there and shaped who you are today.

Ed: Well, to be honest with you, I really never had any ambition to be where I am today. My goal was to provide for my children, so I always worked hard at whatever I did. When opportunities came, I was able to take advantage of them. Usually it was because of an idea, or because of an opportunity, but like I said, the goal was not to be where I am today. I am where I am because I was able to take advantage of various opportunities.

I'm an objectivist and a disciple of the things that Ayn Rand has written through the years. I learned that money is not the reason, money is the reward. Whether you're a doctor, or a scientist, or whatever you may be in life, you do these things because you want to accomplish things and be good at whatever you are doing. Of course you've got to earn a living, but you are not necessarily doing it for that reason. You are doing it because you love what you are doing, and money ends up being the reward.

Perry: What are some of your biggest accomplishments over the years?

Ed: In terms of business, my biggest accomplishment was starting the Philadelphia Flyers as an expansion team when the league expanded from six teams to twelve teams. There are now thirty teams in the National Hockey League. I like to say we're one of the original twelve. Hockey was really almost an unknown thing in Philadelphia at that point. When we started the Flyers, we were designated as the least likely to succeed of the six new teams in the expansion. We were the most successful coming out of the gate.

We had to build an arena, which was called The Spectrum, which was very successful. We took our knowledge and abilities in that business to form a company now known as SMG, which is the largest manager of arenas and stadiums in the world. We formed our own television network in the early days of cable called Prism, which was a big success. We're now in the food concession business and the ticketing business—all things that are interrelated to what we do. We've grown in all kinds of areas, all of which were related to my original jump into hockey.

Perry: During that time, was there ever a crossroads in your career? Was there ever a time when you doubted yourself?

Ed: Well, when I got the franchise from the National Hockey League for the Flyers, I had to mortgage my house and make all kinds of deals to come up with the money to pay the two-million-dollar franchise fee. One night after I had finally raised the money and paid for the franchise, I broke into a cold sweat while talking to my brother-in-law, who was my attorney at the time. I was scared to death that I was crazy. No one knew what hockey was in Philadelphia. I thought maybe I was nuts.

I just thought that it would work. Philadelphia needed an arena for the basketball team, and I was in the forefront of that. I just thought the whole thing would work. I was scared to death, to be honest with you. But it worked . . . beyond my wildest imagination.

Perry: Did you have any mentors? Was there anybody who helped shape you or prepare you to take these risks?

Ed: Well, my greatest inspiration in life was my father, who was an entrepreneur. He succeeded and failed, and succeeded again and failed again. He was up and down, but he was always trying hard to make things work. His primary business when

I was growing up was the grocery business. I was born in our apartment above our grocery store, and then I worked in that grocery store from the time I was eight years old. He always allowed me to make my own decisions, even at that young age. He was a great inspiration, my dad. He always worked hard, and always was up with the next idea.

Perry: Is he the one who helped you get started selling records in grocery stores?

Ed: When I graduated college, my father had joined forces with eight other grocery store owners. There were nine owners altogether of various supermarkets. My father had two stores, and it ended up as a nineteen-store chain.

I got a job upon graduating from college as an advertising manager. My friend and I met a guy at a bar in New York who said he had brand new records from Columbia. I don't even know if you know what they are, but they were 45 RPM records. They could be had for like a penny a piece because they were overlooked. The guy we met said the records were in a warehouse in Carteret, New Jersey. We were intrigued, and we decided that we would figure out something to do with the records.

I then went to my bosses and said, "We can have a record promotion at the stores, and I can see us selling these records [for] nineteen cents each, six for a dollar." Then I went to my father and arranged to have a big record promotion in the nineteen stores of the grocery store chain. We bought up all the records that were in that warehouse, and we had a very successful promotion, but we had a lot of records left over. My friend and I in our spare time decided to sell them to drugstores and other places. We set up racks and started selling them to stores.

Perry: What are your core beliefs and values?

Ed: In the Declaration of Independence, when they talk about the pursuit of happiness—basically, I believe in that. I believe that most people, in my opinion, to be successful, have to really enjoy doing what they're doing. I'm lucky because as a young kid working in my father's grocery store, believe it or not, when he told me I had to mop the floor on a Saturday night, I took great pride in mopping that floor. I loved the fact that it was spotless when I was through. Instead of looking at it as, "Oh my God, I've got to mop the floor," for some reason it didn't bother me. I enjoyed it. I've always enjoyed the things that I've done in life.

I think probably I wouldn't have done them if I didn't enjoy them. I was lucky enough to be able to follow in a path of enjoyment. When I grew older and worked in the stores, and stocked the shelves, was a cashier, or did whatever I had to do, I enjoyed what I was doing. I believe that if you enjoy what you're doing, it's a great leap toward success. It just means that you're really putting everything into it, not because you feel you have to or for the money. You're putting everything into it because you enjoy it.

You love to see things progress and grow, and that's what gives you a thrill. I also believe that you have to balance your career, when you have the opportunity, with your family and with vacations and with all the wonderful things that you want to do in life. Those things help you get rejuvenated to go further, to work harder, and to have more fun.

To give you an example, I love California; it's my favorite place on earth. But I am not able to live there full time because of other opportunities. I go to California because I enjoy it more, and I think it's a wonderful place. However, in the summers in the old days, I used to go to Maine and take my kids there. Now we have a compound and my grown kids and my grandkids all come to the compound that we've developed on a lake in Maine. They spend their summers there, and they love it as much as I did.

Perry: Is there any advice that you would give yourself back when you first started out?

Ed: Well, as you get older, and as you experience success and failure, you learn along the way. The only advice I could give anyone who's entrepreneurial and trying to succeed in life is to learn from your mistakes, and just do it better the next time. In the record business that I told you about, we were so good in the Baltimore/Washington area where we began that the chains that we were working with said, "Well, how about a division in Detroit?" And "How about in Cleveland?" So we expanded, and we grew much larger, but we were young, in our twenties. Basically, we didn't really know how to grow.

We sent our top guys to run divisions in other cities, and we didn't really have the depth to maintain the level of excellence we had when we were smaller. As we grew, we became very ordinary and eventually sold the business—not at any great profit, but simply because we had overextended ourselves, not necessarily financially, but because we didn't know how to train people to manage new divisions. After that, I decided that I didn't ever want to grow too fast, expand too fast, or do things too rapidly when I wasn't prepared to do it. After that, whenever I needed to expand, it was very important that I knew how to, when to, and what I needed to do to manage the expansion successfully.

Perry: Is there anything else that you would like to share, or something important that you think I've missed?

Ed: Well, I believe strongly in the foundation. I believe strongly in the Constitution and the Declaration of Independence. I think this is the greatest country in the world, and I'm a firm believer in capitalism. That is a dirty word among a lot of people in academia and so forth. However, major corporations generally are not capitalists. The capitalists of this country are the entrepreneurs—like yourself, Perry—who are starting small businesses that succeed and maybe even grow into very large businesses. That's what makes this country great.

Perry: We are very blessed to be able to do everything that we do. Thank you for sharing your time and your insights, Ed.

Ed Snider, chairman of Comcast Spectacor, being interviewed early in his career.

Ed Snider with the Stanley Cup. Comcast Spectacor is a Philadelphia-based sports and entertainment company that owns the Philadelphia Flyers. The Flyers became the first NHL expansion team to win the Stanley Cup in 1974, and to repeat as champions in 1975.

Ed Snider was a owner of the Philadelphia Eagles football team in 1964.

Ed Snider with professional hockey legend Gordie Howe who is considered one of the greatest hockey players of all time.

Ed Snider, chairman of Comcast Spectacor. World Cup of Hockey.

Ed Snider with Mike Knuble and Simon Gagne

Ed Snider and the Ed Snider Youth Hockey Foundation.

Ed Snider was entered into the Philadelphia Hall of Fame.

Ed Snider with his family on vacation.

Kai Lenny

Kai is a good friend of mine who is a professional athlete and a fuel-burning machine! He is one of the lucky ones who doesn't have to fit a workout into a busy day because his entire day is a workout, doing the things that he loves to do.

Perry: Tell me a little bit about yourself.

Kai: My name is Kai Lenny. I was born and raised on Maui, Hawaii. I am a professional water athlete who surfs, windsurfs, kitesurfs, stand-up paddles (SUP), big wave surfs—basically anything that involves water, I love to do! I am a five-time SUP World Champion and was runner-up to the Kitesurf World Title in 2013.

Perry: How would some of your close friends describe you?

Kai: I definitely like to have fun, play in the ocean all day long, and eat Taco Bell! I am very passionate about what I do and very competitive. Family is very important to me, and there is no better feeling than riding a really big wave.

Perry: Walk me through a day in your life. What do you eat?

Kai: I try my best to eat as healthy as possible! Sometimes it is really hard when I'm on the road, but I do the best I can once I'm home. I like to have four eggs in the morning for breakfast, chicken and vegetables for lunch, and a big steak and brown rice for dinner. And on occasion I like to get some Taco Bell!

A day for me is waking up at six thirty a.m. and going to Hookipa for a two-hour surf session, followed up by a SUP session. I rush home for a big breakfast, swap out my gear for wind toys, and head back to the beach. First, I windsurf for a couple hours, and then kitesurf as the wind begins to lighten up. To finish the day, I will either do a downwinder on my SUP or go shortboard until the sun falls beneath the mountains.

Perry: Knowing what you know now, what advice would you give yourself back when you first started out?

Kai: I have had such incredible guidance, I feel like I have stuck to the right path and have never veered off it at all. I guess the only advice I would tell myself is that I can handle much more than I realized. It would have been cool to tell myself to charge harder!

Perry: What motivates you?

Kai: My motivations come from my desire to be the best I possibly can. If I have a goal that I want to achieve, I see no reason why I can't do it if I put in the hard work. Since I can remember, I have loved to compete. I always felt it was the best way to push my sport and myself to the next level. Competing just seems to bring the best out of me. To put it simply, I just want to go to the next level. Where the top is, I don't know. All I do know is the higher I climb, the harder it becomes, but the more fulfilling it becomes too!

Perry: What does it take to be successful?

Kai: No matter what, it all comes down to hard work and determination. Sometimes when you can't see the finish line in front of you is when you're the closest to it. It's funny—if you want to win, you have to be willing to sacrifice a lot of things you can't imagine living without, but it is necessary to your cause and your goal. It's just life.

Perry: Describe a time when your workload was heavy and how you handled it.

Kai: Since I do so many different sports, compete on different tours, travel the globe year around, and film for movies and a million other sponsorship promotions, finding time to train can be difficult. I am learning how to do all without using as much energy as before. I did a trip to Patagonia a year ago with two Navy SEALs and three of the top water athletes from Red Bull. We spent two weeks in the middle of nowhere. We would have three to four hours of sleep a night and would mountain climb fifteen miles a day. After that trip, I felt like I could handle twice as much as anything I had experienced.

Perry: What are your thoughts on competition?

Kai: I love competition; I feel like it brings the best out of me. When I get pressed against a wall and it comes down to all or nothing, that's when I am able to tap into the energy held deep within me and show the world what I'm really made of.

Perry: Everyone has weaknesses. How do you suggest dealing with them?

Kai: Like losing an event . . . the only way to overcome your weakness or loss is to look at it straight in the eye with a different set of emotions and thought processes. I try to look inward and become very constructive and understand what it is that I can do to improve. I always try to look forward; whatever has happened has happened. All that matters for me is to do the best I can, to be ready for anything that crosses my path.

Perry: Tell me about some of the things that are most important.

Kai: My family has been a huge part of my success. Without them, I would not be who I am or where I am today. They are so important to me, and that goes for my close circle of friends I consider more like family than anything else. The support team along with my sponsors are just incredible. I like winning for them!

Perry: What is one or some of your biggest accomplishments?

Kai: My biggest accomplishments have been winning eight SUP World Titles (two Race World Titles, four Wave World Titles, and two overall World Titles.) Runner-up Kitesurfing World Title. Winning the Battle of the Paddle back to back in 2013 and 2014. Nomination for Tube of the Year at the Billabong XXL. Alternate spot in the Eddie Aikau Big Wave Invitational. 2009 Rookie of the Year PWA World Windsurfing Tour 2009.

Perry: Many of us struggle with a work/life balance. How do you handle this?

Kai: At this point in my life, everything I do is about being by the ocean, in the ocean, and training to go into the ocean. My entire life is about achieving my dreams and goals. Since my work is my life, it isn't too hard to handle; it's just normal! I still don't feel like I have a job, just the chance to have fun because people like it when I do that!

Perry: Has there been a time when your health was a concern? In those moments, how do priorities change?

Kai: Fortunately I have never had a health condition that has forced me to stop doing what I love or make me reconsider what I'm doing in life. I have had losses of family members, just like everyone experiences in life, and that does open your mind up a bit. My worst injury put me on the couch for one month, and that was when I cut my foot in half after a big wipeout at Jaws. I had to wear a boot and for the first few weeks could not walk at all. It was humbling, but I'm blessed to have come back stronger than ever!

Ed and Kai are both incredibly successful people who took two completely different paths in life. You have your own path and your own definition of success, but I encourage you to make sure fitness is a part of it. You will reach your goals faster and enjoy the process more. Regardless of your definition of success, the most important thing is to make sure you are healthy enough to enjoy the accomplishment of your goals.

Kai Lenny, professional waterman, was born and raised in Hawaii.

Kai Lenny, world-class water athlete, shown here charging the famous wave called Jaws located in Hawaii.

Kai Lenny, World Champion Paddle Boarder.

Kai Lenny at Sunset Beach in 2013.

Kai Lenny paddle surfing.

CONCLUSION

There you have it: the seven success habits recommended by my most successful clients. As we've seen, the first six—create a routine, grow a career from your passion, collaborate, learn from your mistakes, lead from within, and set meaningful goals—are tried-and-true success principles most anyone would agree with. But we rarely hear about the seventh—sweat every day—even though it's just as foundational to our success both at work and in life. In fact, the most success-driven individuals (some might call them "workaholics") tend to be the most resistant to working out, and our work environments still tend to encourage and reward sitting and working long hours.

If you don't have a regular workout routine, and you're beginning to think that working out may be exactly what you need to get to the next

3. **Collaborate.** Assemble a great team of professionals to help you accomplish your fitness goals. Involve your doctor. Consult a trainer and a nutritionist. Go to a physical therapist if you are struggling with an injury. Treat yourself to a massage every once in a while. Assemble a team of peers to share the journey to fitness. Get a running partner. Join a club or team sport. Go to a fitness class. If you make it social, you will be less likely to be a no-show.

4. **Learn from your mistakes.** Hopefully your mistakes will not be as dramatic as mine, but you will make them, and you should learn from them all the same. You will overdo it, but learn to listen to your body. You may get injured, but you will work through it and learn to prevent injury in the future.

5. **Lead from within.** Exercise forces you to practice your leadership skills on the most difficult and reluctant of followers –yourself. You won't be able to effectively lead others until you can lead yourself, so lead your ass out of bed and to the gym.

6. **Set meaningful goals.** Nothing is more important to a successful exercise routine than meaningful goals. Again, Part Two of this book is always there for you to refer back to; there is no need for you to reinvent the wheel. It really is just a matter of taking action every day and not giving up.

And if you need further support, I encourage you to:

*   Visit my website at www.workoutandgrowrich.com
*   For corporate wellness needs, visit www.foundwellness.com.
*   Visit our gym, The Workplace, if you're in the Santa Barbara, CA, area: www.workplacesb.com.

Finally, if working out really was the missing link to growing rich for you, I'd love to hear about it. Share your stories on Twitter @ foundwellnessco, on Facebook, or e-mail me at <u>foundwellness@me.com</u>.

BONUS RESISTANCE TRAINING WORKOUTS

Below are six bonus resistance training workouts: two beginner workouts, two moderate workouts, and two advanced workouts. See my website for video instructions about how to perform the exercises: www.workoutandgrowrich.com. And keep checking back for more bonus material and workouts!

Beginner Workout 1
Warm-Up
- Use Basic Warm-Up or a variation of your own

Core (2 times through)
- Frankenstein Roll-Ups: 10 reps
- Teaser Crunch Hold: 15 seconds per leg
- Russian Twist: 15 reps per side
- Front Plank Hold: 30-second hold

Strength Circuit One (3 times through)
- Pull-Ups or Pull-Up Negatives: 2 reps
- Reverse Lunge (right leg only): 8 reps
- Pull-Ups or Pull-Up Negatives: 2 reps
- Reverse Lunge (left leg only): 8 reps
- Push-Ups: 12 reps

Strength Circuit Two (3 times through)
- Shoulder Press with Dumbbell or Kettlebell (right arm): 4 reps
- Hip-Up Bridge: 8 reps
- Shoulder Press with Dumbbell or Kettlebell (left arm): 4 reps
- Hip-Up Bridge: 8 reps
- Squat Rows with Band or Cable Machine: 12 reps

Cardio Intervals (2 times through)
Pick your machine:
- 4 x 30 seconds at 85 percent effort with 30-second recovery
- 1-minute recovery
- 2 minutes at 75–85 percent effort, then 1-minute recovery

Beginner Workout 2
Warm-Up
- Use Basic Warm-Up or a variation of your own

Core (2 times through)
- Frankenstein Roll-Ups: 10 reps
- Teaser Crunch Hold: 15 seconds per leg
- Front Plank Hold: 30-second hold
- Frankenstein Roll-Ups: 10 reps
- Russian Twist: 15 reps per side
- Side Plank Hold: 30 second hold per side

Strength Circuit One (4 times through)
- Incline Dumbbell Press: right arm 1 rep, left arm 1 rep, and both arms 1 rep, for a total of 6 reps
- Weighted Side Lunges: 6 per side
- Front Plank Twist: 10 reps per side

Strength Circuit Two (4 times through)
- Assisted Pull-Ups: 6 reps
- Weighted Reverse Lunges: 6 per leg
- Frankenstein Roll-Ups: 10 reps

Strength Circuit Three (4 times through)
- Push-Ups (assisted if needed): 6 reps
- Squat Row with Band or Cable Machine: 12 reps
- Side Plank Hold (with feet on bench): 30-second hold per side

Strength Circuit Four (4 times through, 8 minutes)
Start each jump on the 30-second mark.
- Squat Jumps: 10 reps
- Split Jumps: 10 reps per side
- Burpees: 5 reps
- Ice Skater Jumps: 10 reps per side

Cardio Intervals

For time, complete all of the following:

- ½ mile on the elliptical at 85 percent effort
- 1,000 meter row at 85 percent effort
- ½ mile run or walk at 85 percent effort

Moderate Workout 1 (1 hour with warm-up)

Warm-Up

- Use Basic Warm-Up or a variation of your own

Core (2 times through or 8 minutes)

- Reverse Crunches on Bench: 15 reps
- Walk-Outs from Push-Up Position: 5 reps, hold each one out for 3 seconds
- Back Extension: 15 reps into back extension, hold with arms up for 15 seconds
- Side Plank Hold (raise top leg up): 30-second hold per leg

Strength Circuit One (3 times through or 8 minutes)

- Pull-Ups: 4 reps
- Weighted Step-Ups into a Reverse Lunge: 4 per leg
- Push-Ups: 8 reps
- Single Leg Hamstring Bridge Raises: 8 per leg

Strength Circuit Two (3 times through or 8 minutes)

- Arnold Presses with Dumbbells: 4 reps
- Weighted Single-Leg Squats: 4 reps per leg (3 seconds down, 2-second hold at bottom, 1-second up)
- Single-Arm Weighted Row: 8 per arm
- Weighted Side Lunges: 8 per side

Strength Circuit Three (10 minutes)

- Grab two kettlebells, one heavier than the other. On the 1-minute mark, you will swing the heavier kettlebell for 10 reps, followed directly by the lighter one for 15 reps—the quicker you finish, the more time you have to recover. Repeat cycle for 10 rounds/10 minutes.

Cardio Intervals

Choose an option:
- All-out for time, elliptical: 1 mile
- All-out for time, rower: 2,000 meters
- All-out for time, ski erg: 2,000 meters
- All-out for time, run: 1 mile

Moderate Workout 2

Warm-Up

- Use Basic Warm-Up or a variation of your own

Core (1 time through)

- Frankenstein Roll-Ups: 10 reps
- Russian Twist: 15 per side
- Frankenstein Roll-Ups: 10 reps
- Teaser Crunches: 15 per side
- Frankenstein Roll-Ups: 10 reps
- Leg Lifts: 15 reps
- Side Planks: 10 dips, 10 scoops, and 10-second leg lift (hold per side)
- Frankenstein Roll-Ups: 10 reps
- Front Plank Hold: 1 minute

Strength Circuit One (2 times through or 16 minutes)
- Pull-Ups: 3 reps
- Decline Push-Ups: 6 reps
- Pull-Ups: 3 reps
- Yoga Push-Ups: 6 reps
- Pull-Ups: 3 reps
- Medicine Ball Push-Ups: 3 per hand
- Rower or Ski Erg: 4 minutes at 75 percent

Strength Circuit Two (2 times through or 16 minutes)
- Deadlifts with Kettlebells or Dumbbells: 3 reps
- Weighted Step-Ups: 6 reps per leg
- Deadlifts with Kettlebells or Dumbbells: 3 reps
- Weighted Squat Doubles: 6 reps
- Deadlifts with Kettlebells or Dumbbells: 3 reps
- Weighted Side Lunges: 6 reps per side
- Elliptical: 4 minutes at 75 percent

Advanced Workout 1
Warm-Up
- Use Basic Warm-Up or a variation of your own

Core: 2 times through
- Turkish Get-Ups: 2 per side
- Ab Wheel: 5 reps with 2-second hold on each rep
- Straight-Legged Hanging Leg Raise: 5 reps
- Band Punches and Chops: 10 punches, then 15 chops per side

Strength Circuit One (8 minutes)
- Barbell or Dumbbell Clean and Press: 7 reps
- Mission Impossible Rows: 15 reps

Strength Circuit Two (8 minutes)
- Weighted Step-Ups on Box or Bench: 7 reps per leg
- Kettlebell Swings: 15 reps

Strength Circuit Three (8 minutes)
- Pull-Ups: 7 reps
- Incline Dumbbell Bench Press: 15 doubles (all the way down, up a little, back down, then all the way up)

Strength Circuit Four (8 minutes)
- Weighted Side Lunges: 7 per side
- Weighted Front Squats with Dumbbells or Kettlebells: 15 reps

Strength Circuit Five (8 minutes)
- Full Sit-Ups: 15 reps
- Push-Up Ball Roll (with shins on balance ball): 7 reps

Cardio Intervals (8–10 minutes)
- Repeat the following 4 times: 250 meter row at 90 percent effort, then immediately move to the elliptical at resistance 10 for 30 seconds as fast as you can with your arms straight up, then 45-second recovery

Advanced Workout 2 (1 hour with warm-up)
Warm-Up
- Use Basic Warm-Up or a variation of your own

Strength Circuit One (3 to 4 times through or 10 minutes)
- Kettlebell Squat Doubles (semi-heavy): 4 reps
- Kettlebell Swings: 12 reps (men 44 lbs., women 30 lbs.)
- Dumbbell Single Arm Lunge and Press: 4 reps per arm

- Plyo/Clapping Push-Ups (use band or bench, or stay on knees for assistance): 8 reps

Strength Circuit Two (3 to 4 times through or 10 minutes)
- Plyo Pull-Ups: 4 reps (use band if needed)
- Normal Pull-Ups: 4 reps
- Lunge Cable Row (Sassy Row): 8 per arm
- Barbell, Kettlebell, or Dumbbell Deadlifts: 4 reps
- Kettlebell Snatches: 8 per arm

Strength Circuit Three (2 to 3 times through)
- Weighted V-Ups on Bench: 12 reps
- Bicycles Crunches on Bench: 12 per side
- Roll-Outs on Rower Seat: 12 reps with 5-second hold on each one
- Weighted Russian Twist: 12 per side
- Band Punches and Chops: 10 punches/15 chops per side

Strength Circuit Four (4 times through or 10 minutes)
- Jumps on the 30-second mark:
- Squat Jumps: 15 reps
- Medicine Ball Slams: 15 reps
- Ice Skater Jumps: 10 per side
- Burpees with Push-Up: 5 reps
- Split Jumps: 10 reps per side

Cardio Intervals (1 time through)
- On elliptical at resistance 8, 9, or 10: 20 seconds hard (90 percent), then 40 seconds easy (repeat 4 times)
- 1,000 meters on the rower at 80 percent (1 time)

ACKNOWLEDGMENTS

To my incredible and supportive family—my loving wife, Nora, who always supports me no matter what I do and always takes the time to hear me vent and points me in the right direction. And to my daughter, Sage—thank you for being my everything and for making me a happier person.

To Greg Renker, whose friendship and association have opened my eyes to new possibilities of what my career can become. Your relentless dedication, energy, and words of wisdom inspire me more than you know.

To Brian Donahoo, one of my first clients and the one who helped encourage and direct me to going out on my own and starting Foundwellness. You have been a huge influence in my life for the past ten years, and I hope for many more to come.

To my team of people and other trainers I work with—thank you all for being mentors to me and sharing your knowledge and ideas. Our collaborations have made me look at training and life in a different light, and I cannot wait to see what the future brings.

ABOUT THE AUTHOR

Elite personal trainer and president of Foundwellness: The Workplace Workout, Perry Lieber is a proven expert in bringing wellness to the workplace and fueling peak performance at the highest level.

Perry received his bachelor's degree from the University of California, Santa Barbara, during which time he completed his first Ironman competition. After more than ten years of personal training expertise with some of America's most influential and successful people, including professional athletes such as Al Horford of the Atlanta Hawks, Kyle Singler of the Oklahoma City Thunder, pro waterman Kai Lenny, business professionals such as Ed Snider, Greg Renker, and Andy Puzder, and celebrities such as Glenn Frey, lead singer of The Eagles, he discovered that each of these clients had their own story of what it takes to be successful.

Through these relationships, Perry's vision for Foundwellness took shape: taking the common challenges that we all face and creating programs that promote a sustainable lifestyle and allow us to reach our dreams of success. Today, Foundwellness helps businesses create healthy work cultures through onsite workouts, nutrition education, and online resources, all specifically targeted toward peak performance at work.

Perry is a member of the National Academy of Sports Medicine and, in 2012, opened his own elite training facility called The Workplace. He continues to compete in everything from paddle boarding to running and cycling events. Today, corporate clients join in these events as Perry helps them set goals and establish milestones so that participation is fun, competitive, and healthy.

FURTHER RESOURCES

For more information about Workbody Training programs, including getting certified:

www.workandgrowrich.com

Do you own or work for a company that wants to create a better, more successful work culture? Start thriving today. For more information about Foundwellness Training, classes, testimonials, and on-demand workout videos:

www.foundwellness.com

The Workplace provides goal-oriented, performance-driven workout regimens to suit everyone's needs.

www.workplacesb.com